SIENA

and its province

by *Enzo Carli*

editions **ITALCARDS** bologna - italy

Sole distributor for Siena and its province
C.N.C.
Località Valcanoro ☎ 055/80.78.424
Barberino Val d'Elsa (FI)

Graphics and Pagination:

Federico Frassinetti

Photography:

Ascanio Ascani - Misano (Fo),
Foto Studio Gielle Siena - Federico Frassinetti
Foto Barone - Firenze
Ezio Quiresi - Cremona
Foto Lenzini - Siena

Editions ITALCARDS bologna - italy

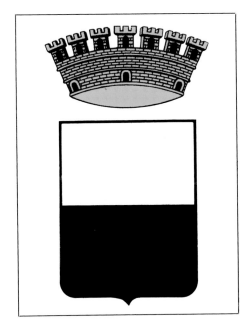

HISTORICAL BACKGROUND AND TOWN DEVELOPMENT

The origin of the name of Siena is explained by a poetic legend, which also throws light on the meaning of its civic insignia: a Roman she-wolf feeding two children and a bipartite, black and white coat of arms popularly called «Balzana». In fact, ancient historians report that Senio and Aschio, the two young sons of Remus, suspected by Romulus after their father had been killed, fled from Rome carrying with the revered simulacrum of the she-wolf as a good omen for them and which they had stolen from the temple of Apollo. Pursued by Romulus' emissaries, the two brothers were about to be captured when two beautiful horses, a white one and a black one, appeared to them during a storm and carried them to a place on the banks of a stream, the Tressa, where they were finally able to rest. There, they erected a temple dedicated to Apollo and, on an overlooking hill, a castle, which represented the original centre of today's town. Today «Castel Senio» or «Castel Vecchio» is still the name of a group of houses in the highest part of the town, near via Stalloreggi, a street which also testifies, through its Latin name coming from *Stallum regii*, of the earliest events concerning Siena. According to another legend, however, the town was founded by the *Senones* or *Senes Galli* who stopped there on their way to Rome during the invasion in the 5th century B.C. At any rate, some finds datable back to the 2nd and 1st centuries, and the town's name as well, probably coming from that of a powerful Etruscan family from Chiusi, *Saina*, later Latinized to *Saena*, prove that Siena was an Etruscan centre.

During the Republican period Siena came under Roman rule and around 20 B.C. Augustus founded there a military colony. It is not possible to know the exact extension of the Roman town, which was supplied by an aqueduct and had at least four gates and a temple devoted to Diana, now completely destroyed: some archeological finds, however, lead us to think that its size was greater than in the early Middle Ages, when it shrunk in size and population and was mainly concentrated on the hills of Castelvecchio and Santa Maria.

According to tradition, Christianity became widespread in Siena between the end of the 3rd century and the beginning of the 4th thanks to Ansano, of the Roman family Anicia, who was martyrized there in 303 and who is considered the first patron saint of the town. Towards the middle of the 5th century, a Bishop's seat was established in Siena; suppressed for several decades during the Langobard invasions, it was restored by Rotari in the middle of the 7th century. Under the Langobard rule the town was governed by Gastaldi (administrators of royal demesnes), who were replaced, after the French conquest, by Counts, and, from the 7th to the 11th centuries, the centre developed along the *Romean Way*, also called *Francigena*, the most important communication link between Italy and Northern Europe. The road followed to-

day's street layout and, coming from the North, passed through Camollia, where in Roman times a «villa» stood, later a suburb, and then led to via Montanini and to the Banchi di Sotto. Finally it turned to the south-east along via del Porrione, towards Porta Romana, leaving the original centre of Castelvecchio and Santa Maria on its right. Around this layout the town's characteristic planimetry took form, which has survived until now, in the shape of an upside-down Y whose three arms correspond to the three «terzi» or «terzieri», the districts into which the town was, and is, divided: «Città», to the south-west, is the oldest part of town; then «S. Martino», to the south-east, and «Camollia», to the north-west. Among humble houses, made of tufaceous rock and various building materials, the «castellari», constructions of stone and brick where the families of the feudal aristocracy lived, began to dot the Sienese landscape; these families were often of Germanic origin, like, for example, the Salimbeni and the Malavolti, who are said to have been founded by knights who came to Italy with Charlemagne in 796. The new groups of houses which grew along the via Francigena and which were then isolated from one another, had each a church: among them we can still recall S. Martino, after which a «terziere» had been named, S. Cristoforo, S. Giorgio, S. Paolo and S.

Municipal Museum: Sienese she-wolf, by Giovanni di Turino.

Donato: other ones were built in the 10th century after an increase in the population. The earliest Bishop's seat had probably been located in the Roman «oppidum» of Castelvecchio, a fortified town, although it must have been moved to its present position during the 9th century, because that location was mentioned for the first time in 913. The first Cathedral of the town was erected next to it and later the 1058 Council was housed there: probably its layout was originally perpendicular to today's church and its façade looked onto via del Capitano (perhaps the ancient «decumanus»). During the first half ot the 12th century a new church was built: it was consecrated in 1179 but it was widely rebuilt around the middle of the 13th century. The church, together with the Spedale (hospital) which was founded during the 10th century and enlarged starting from the end of the 12th century onwards for the next two centuries, determined the earliest urban configuration of that area called «piano di Santa Maria» (Santa Maria flat land). The power of the Bishops began to grow in the 10th century: between 1053 and 1056, after subjugating some of the great feudatories, they received by emperor Henry III of Franconia the legitimization of their temporal power on the town and on the bishopric estate. The government of the town was held at first by the Bishop together with imperial Counts; later, as the power of the higher classes who had allied with the common people grew

stronger, Counts were replaced by three Consuls, two of whom were chosen among the noblemen and one among the people. In 1147 Count-Bishop Raniero was forced to leave the town where a civilian government was established, thus giving rise to a free City-State. During that period, in spite of frequent and bitter internecine disputes between noblemen and rich merchants, as well as between merchants and the lower classes, the territory of Siena was considerably enlarged to the detriment of the nearby feudatories who were hindering trade through customs and tolls. In opposition to Florence which was a Guelph town, Siena took sides with the Ghibelline faction. The rivalry between Siena and Florence, however, was caused, rather than by political reasons, by contrasting economic interests, Florence being the chief commercial competitor of Siena, in which a class of merchants, bound to reach their highest expansion in the following century, had taken roots since the middle of the 12th century. The rich merchants and bankers of Siena, such as the Malavolti, the Tolomei, the Piccolomini and the Saracini among the town's leading figures, were then doing business in many places of Europe and the Near East. During the first half of the 13th century, they became also the most important bankers of the Apostolic See. The struggle with Florence continued with ups and downs, culminating in the famous battle of Montaperti, where the Sienese Ghibelline led by Provenzano

Salvani and by the leader of the Florentine exiles, Farinata degli Uberti, and helped by the knights of King Manfred of Swabia and by the allies of Lucca, Pisa and Cortona, inflicted, on 4 September 1260, a bloody defeat on the Guelphs of Florence. The battle was recalled by Dante as «lo strazio e il grande scempio - che fece l'Arbia colorata in rosso» (Big massacre and torment which made the river Arbia turn red). The victory, marking the triumph of the Ghibelline faction in Tuscany, was however of little advantage to Siena which was excommunicated by the Pope, who also, by stopping to be a customer of its bankers, set an example followed by many of the bankers' debtors, who then refused to pay up.

In 1190 the Consuls were replaced by a Podesta, to whom were added later the Council of the Twenty-four, a body formed by twelve representatives of the people and twelve Ghibelline noblemen, and a Capitano del Popolo (a commander of the local militia) in 1252. After the defeat at Colle Val d'Elsa the Government of the Thirty-six (1271-1280), belonging to the Guelph faction, then of the Fifteen (1280-1286) and finally of the Nine, or «Noveschi», was subsequently established. The last one remained in office from 1287 to

1355, following a Guelph policy and establishing friendly relations with Florence. It was the best government of the town, under which Siena reached a considerable prosperity and was endowed with its most important monuments, like for example the Palazzo Pubblico (Public Palace); moreover, the construction of the massive «Duomo Nuovo», although never completed, was begun in 1339, and, with the aid of the town's authorities, the big churches of monastic orders like those of S. Francesco, S. Domenico, S. Clemente ai Servi, S. Agostino and S. Niccolò al Carmine, all of them standing on the edge of the ancient town centre, were built or enlarged. That period had also been marked by an extraordinary flowering of art-works, particularly in painting, with masters like Duccio di Boninsegna, Simone Martini, the brothers Lorenzetti and their followers, who established a «school», which soon became one of the most important and original in Europe. In 1326, the town walls were enlarged and reached their present size, apart from a short stretch which was added in 1401 below the cloister of S. Francesco: since then the buildings' layout in the centre of town has practically remained unchanged. Wars, a famine in 1326 and the Black Death of 1348, however, created a difficult situation even for the Noveschi

who were overthrown and replaced by the Twelve (1355), and later (1368) by the Fifteen Reformers, all of them coming from the humble people and ruling until 1386. Other forms of government followed, although of short duration due to unstable relations among the social classes, so that Siena, maybe tired of struggles, gave itself up to Gian Galeazzo Visconti in 1399, declaring him its Seigneur. During those unruly days the great figure of Caterina Benincasa (1347-1380) emerged, a woman imploring peace among factions, as Bernardino degli Albizzeschi (1380-1444) did later. After Visconti's death a government, called of the Ten Priors, was established, mainly formed by persons taken from the common people ; then, together with Alfonso Duke of Calabria, who had contributed to the defeat of the Florentine at Poggio Imperiale (1479), the rich bourgeoisie returned to power, with the support of the people, with the old Noveschi who, banished in 1482, succeeded in suddenly entering the town in 1487 under the guide of Pandolfo Petrucci. He ruled from 1502 to 1512 as an absolute sovereign, recovering the economy and fostering the arts; on the contrary, his sons Borghese and Fabio, who had succeeded him, were forced to leave town, which was held for a short time by Alessandro Bichi, the leader of the Nine, later killed during a riot of the «Libertine» (popular party). This aroused the anger of Pope Clement VII, who, being favourable to the Nine, sent a whole army to fight against Sie-

na: the papal troops, however, were defeated outside Camollia gate on 25 July 1526. In 1531, on the pretext of pacifying the opposite factions, Charles V ordered the town to be garrisoned and, in 1547, his vicar don Diego Hurtado de Mendoza had many of its towers demolished or lowered to obtain the building materials for a fortress. This was pulled to pieces in 1552, when the Spanish were thrown out by the Sienese people who formed an alliance with France and with the Florentine exiles led by Piero Strozzi. The Spanish, however, were eager to take revenge and Cosimo I de' Medici, the Seigneur of Florence who wanted the town, pushed Charles V to retaliation: in 1553 a Spanish army led by Don Garcia Toledo plundered the Sienese territory. The following year, in March, twenty-four thousand Spanish and Florentine soldiers led by Gian Giacomo de' Medici, Marquess of Marignano, besieged the town. The Sienese people, guided by Biagio di Montluc and helped by a small French garrison army, tried for over one year to defend their freedom with epic strenuousness. The heroic courage of the besieged was proved by a number of episodes: battalions of women effectively contributed to repulse the invaders and the struggle only ended when, after driving out all the useless mouths to feed, after using all available means, from plants to animals, and after running out of ammunition, the people had nothing more left to feed themselves and to fight with. The culverin shot, which on one morning in April 1555 broke the pole of the «Balzana» waving over the Torre (tower) del Mangia, signed the setting for the town's freedom. On 17 April Siena surrendered to the enemy, but more than 650 families preferred the exile in Montalcino to the servitude under Strozzi. There, they set up the seat of the Republic and held it for four years continuing to mint coins with the glorious symbol of their lost native land, until 15 July 1559 when, ac-

1. Aerial view of Siena; 2. 3. Partial views from the Torre del Mangia; 4. Panoramic view of the Cathedral and the Duomo Nuovo from above; 5. Detail of Porta Romana.

cording to the treaty of Câteau-Cambresis, Siena was included into the dominion of the Medici as a feud of the Spanish crown, except for the ports of the Tyrrhenian Sea belonging to the Sienese territory, which formed the «Stato dei Presìdi» (State of the Garrisons) under the vice-royalty of Naples. On 30 October 1560, Cosimo I de' Medici made his solemn entrance into Siena, joyfully welcomed by the population who, exhausted by the siege, had been reduced to slightly more than 10,000 inhabitants from about the previous 22,500. The town was given an independent government formed by a Governatore (governor), a Concistoro (assembly) and the Balìa (body of judges with extraordinary power), and, under the Medici rule, civic life began to bloom again. The population increased sensibly, new imposing churches were built, like S. Maria di Provenzano (1595), and many of them were restored, like S. Martino and S. Vigilio; the Governor's Palace was built on Piazza del Duomo, on the place where the old houses of the Petrucci family had once stood and Chigi-Zonzadari Palace, as well as the back of the Merchants' Loggia, were given new façades, while the two lateral wings of Public Palace were raised by a floor in 1680-81. In 1561 the reconstruction of the Fortress of S. Barbara, with its powerful angular bastions, was also begun. After the Medici, Siena, as the whole region of Tuscany, passed under the rule of the Lorraine fa-

mily, to whom it returned after the period of the Napoleonic domination, during which it was the administrative centre of the Ombrone district. In 1852 it was the first Tuscan town to choose, by general agreement, the annexation to the kingdom of Italy.

Famous sienese people

A number of famous persons in the field of religion, literature, science and politics were born in Siena, beside the already mentioned wide group of great artists who made the name of Siena known everywhere in the world. We have already mentioned St. Catherine, the Virgin of Fontebranda who was elected Italy's Patron Saint (1247-1380), and St. Bernardino, who, although born in Massa Marittima, was a Sienese by family and upbringing (1380-1444): among the numerous Blessed ones, the best known are Ambrogio Sansedoni, Andrea Gallerani and Pier Pettinaio, who lived in the 13th century and was remembered by Dante; Bernardo Tolomei, the founder of the Order of the Olivetan Benedictine, Giovanni Colombini, the founder of the «Gesuati» and Filippo degli Agazzari, the author of the «Assempri», a collection of votive short stories and a precious example of Italian language, in the 14th century. Among the Popes who were born in Siena, or were raised there at least three are remembered for their par-

ticularly brilliant pontificate: Alexander III (Rolando Bandinelli, elected in 1159, died 1181), the founder of the Lombard League which defeated Barbarossa; Pius II (Enea Silvio Piccolomini, 1405-1464), a famous humanist, a writer and a politician, and Alexander VII (Fabio Chigi, 1599-1667), whose name is related to the grandiose Bernini architecture in the Vatican. As a counterpoint to that, one of the most learned and fervent supporters of Protestantism, Bernardino Tommasini, called «Bernardino Ochino» (after the Contrada dell'Oca, the Goose district of Siena: 1487 - Slavkov in Moravia 1564), as well as philosophers and freethinkers like Lelio (1525 - Zurich 1562) and Fausto Socini (1539 - Cracow 1604), the founders of «Socianism», a doctrine which had followers in Europe up to the beginning of the 19th century, were also born in Siena.

In the history of Italian literature a significant place is held by the poet Cecco Angiolieri (ca.1258-1312), the author of 150 sonnets in vulgar Italian, free of prejudices and of a keen caustic inspiration; mention should also be made of Lu-

Palazzo Pubblico, Sala della Pace (Hall of Peace): 1. Detail of the Effects of Good Government in the town, by Ambrogio Lorenzetti; 2. Room of the Mappamondo (world map): the «Battle of the Sienese against the Florentine at Poggio Imperiale», fresco by Giovanni di Cristoforo and Francesco di Andrea (1480); 3. Sala di Balìa: «Naval battle between the Venetians and the Imperial troops at Punta Salvore», by Spinello Aretino (detail).

2

dovico Sergardi («Quinto Settano», 1660-1726) for his 18 «Satire» in Latin, and Girolamo Gigli (1660-1722), a bright polemic writer, supporter of the superiority of the Sienese idiom over the Florentine one, and a brilliant playwright and scholar. In the field of history Siena counts a great number of scholars, going, almost uninterruptedly, from the primitive chroniclers of the 14th century to the 17th-century ones, mainly devoted to local history. Gaetano Milanesi (1813-1895), a careful collector of documents on Sienese art, is also to be mentioned for a major annotated edition of Vasari's «Lives». A great economist, Sallustio Bandini (1677-1770) and the botanist and physician Pier Andrea Mattioli (1500-1577) were also very famous. In more recent times Siena was honoured by the names of Federico Tozzi (1883-1920), a powerful and tormented novelist, among the greatest of our century, and of Ranuccio Bianchi Bandinelli (1900-1975), a famous archaeologist and a critic of ancient art. Together with the University, dating back to the 13th century, there are also other very active cultural centres such as the Intronati Academy, founded in 1525 for research in the fields of history and literature, and the Chigiana Musical Academy which, founded in 1931 by count Guido Chigi Saracini (1880-1965), has become well established as the most important specialization school for composers at an international level.

3

There are just a few towns in the world which can boast as remarkable and precious an artistic heritage as Siena does, all inside the narrow circle of its red walls. And this is particularly striking if one thinks that the town was neither favoured by an enlightened patronage of noble families, like the Medici of Florence or the Dukes of Urbino, nor had passed through periods of absolute economic prosperity: on the contrary, its life was accompanied for centuries with the

SIENESE ART

Architecture • Sculpture • Painting • Other arts

crashing of arms, it was always tormented by the struggle between factions and often impoverished by wars and sieges, let alone the ruin caused by plagues and famines. It was mainly the passion and ambition of the different social classes, the people's religious faith and their instinctive and fervent love for every form of beauty which made it possible for a quite original artistic tradition to develop and become established in Siena so that wonderful masterpieces could flower in churches, palaces and museums, where they still astonish and enrapture tourists today.

Architecture

Sienese architecture reached its apex and autonomous features during the Gothic period: the few Romanesque buildings still preserved in town, in fact, like the apse and the cloister of S. Cristoforo, the church of S. Pietro alla Magione, of S. Donato, S. Andrea and S. Maria in Bethlhem, do not reveal any original feature, even though they show

some elements of the Lombard architecture, modified with a certain gracefulness, like the ornamentation with airy, sometimes intertwined, small arches. The surrounding countryside, on the contrary, offers a remarkable and wide choice of Romanesque churches, such as the famous Abbey of S. Antimo in Castelnuovo dell'Abate near Montalcino, which stands out for its extraordinary beauty and for its importance in the history of architecture. The Abbey was built in the 12th century by monks who had studied the building methods of Burgundy. Civil architecture in the Romanesque period is represented by some «towerhouses» of stone, like the one standing near the church of S. Ansano and that of the Forteguerri family, in Postierla square from the 12th century. During the following century the Sienese territory set the tone for a general renewal of religious architecture all over Tuscany: the imposing ruins of the abbatial church of S. Galgano, which rises in the lonely valley of the Merse river, are in fact among the earliest expressions of an Italian application of the Gothic style across the Alps. The church, built between 1224 and 1288 by Cistercian monks on the

spot where Galgano Guidotti, knight of Chiusdino canonized in 1185, had lived as a hermit, was an example for all the Tuscan churches of the 13th and 14th centuries. Shortly after the mid-13th century the interior of the Church was rebuilt, perhaps by Nicola Pisano, over the previous place of worship, consecrated in 1179. The dome was covered with lead in 1263, the nave and aisles of the front body were built in a later period and show a transition style between Romanesque and Gothic. The façade, after a drawing by Giovanni Pisano, and the extension of the choir, with the S. Giovanni underneath it, begun in 1317 under the guide of Camaino di Crescentino, are in Gothic style. In 1339, the works at the huge mass of the «Duomo Nuovo», the Cathedral, a grandiose enterprise at which Giovanni d'Agostino also worked, were started but were to be interrupted in 1348. The «Duomo Nuovo», although unfinished, expresses with an absolute, unmistakable originality the features of the Sienese religious architecture of the Gothic period, with its highest peaks both in its space structure and in the refinement of its decorations. However, the big churches of the men-

tain) date back to the first half of the 14th century, although the latter was widely restored in the 19th century. Palazzo Marsili and Palazzo Bonsignori are the best known examples of Gothic style from the mid-15th century. Mention should be also made of the typical architecture of fountains, which consist of wide basins of stone and bricks covered by cross-vaults, as we can see in the oldest one, the Fonte Branda, and in the Fonte Nuova and Fonte di Pescaia. Another typical Gothic feature in Sienese architecture is represented by the gates of the town walls, made of bricks, with barbicans and battlements, like Porta Romana, Porta Pispini, Porta Ovile and the grandiose Antiporto (outside gate) of Camollia.

Gothic and Renaissance styles are harmoniously mixed in the Merchants' Loggia from the beginning of the 15th century, enriched with sculptures during the second half of that century, and in the 14th-century Chapel of Piazza, to which crowning arches were added by Antonio Federighi (died ca.1490), a sculptor and architect to whom we owe also the airy Pope's Logge and the picturesque Devil's Palace. In that period, themes from the Florentine Renaissance style came to be established here, and are now to be seen in Piccolomini Palace and in the other Piccolomini Palace also called «Palace of the Papesse (women-Popes)», both probably built according to a plan by Bernardo Rossellino; in Spannocchi Palace, begun by Giuliano da Maiano, and in S. Galgano Palace, dedicated to that Saint. The greatest military architect of the 15th century, Francesco di Giorgio Martini (1439-1502) was born in Siena and was very active in several Italian regions, from the Marches to Tuscany, from

dicant orders like S. Francesco and S. Domenico, built during the 13th cent. and enlarged during the 14th cent., as well as the Carmine Church from the 14th cent., with only one wide nave, truss roofing and fired-brick floor, are in no way dissimilar to those of the monastic architecture. Civil architecture, both public and private, is in Siena very important and every square and street of the town centre show remarkable examples of it, often very well preserved. Siena, in fact, from the 13th cent. to the first half of the 15th cent., took on that typical look which is still today one of its major attractions. Almost all the civic buildings show, in recurring elements,

the so-called «Sienese arch», formed by a blind depressed arch, surmounted by a falcate ogive. The somewhat primitive tower-houses and gloomy buildings with sparse windows are followed by sumptuous palaces with façades enlivened by series of airy and charming three- or two-light mullioned windows with pointed arches, and garlanded by a battlement supported by corbels in the shape of upside-down pyramids. The highest expression of that elegant style is the Palazzo del Comune (Town Hall), rightly considered the most beautiful among Italy's public buildings from the Gothic period. The oldest private building is Tolomei Palace, rebuilt towards the end of the 13th century with its graceful façade made entirely out of stone. The Sansedoni and Chigi-Saracini palaces and that of the Capitano del Popolo (People's Cap-

1. State archives: Good Government in the Tax Office, by Benvenuto di Giovanni; 2. Via San Pietro; 3. Façade of the Duomo; 4. Via di città.

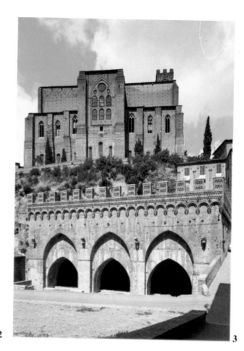

Carthusian brother Damiano Schifardini, and under the guide of Flaminio del Turco (died 1634), who built also the beautiful church of SS. Pietro e Paolo. Some examples of 18th-century architecture are also to be seen in Siena, like the façade of the church of S. Vigilio and the renewed interior of the Gothic church of S. Agostino by Luigi Vanvitelli. The 19th century is characterized by the local, openly «puristic» current, marked by the intense activity of Giuseppe Partini (1842-1895).

Sculpture

Sculptures dating back to the Romanesque period are scanty and are to be found mostly in the countryside. A great plastic tradition was initiated in Siena in the building site of the Duomo shortly after the mid-13th century by Nicola Pisano, who, after decorating the interior of the dome's drum with magnificent heads, carried out, between 1265 and 1268, together with his son Giovanni, Arnolfo di Cambio and others, that extraordinary pulpit which represents one of the greatest masterpieces in Medieval European sculpture. The imposing sculpted capitals of the front body belong to the school of Nicola Pisano, and Giovanni Pisano worked from 1284 to 1297 at the façade, animating it with a series of big statues representing figures from the Bible and from the classical world in dramatic attitudes, which stand

Lombardy to Naples and Siena; he worked at the enlargement of the church of S. Francesco and at the rebuilding of the Osservanza Basilica, in which his pupil Giacomo Cozzarelli (1453-1515), probably the architect of Petruccio Palace, also called «Palace of the Magnifico», also took part. During the 16th century Siena had another great architect, Baldassarre Peruzzi (1481-1536), whose style parted from Bramante's pictorially perspective ideas by recalling Raphael's architectural works. Back in Siena after having worked in Rome (villa «la Farnesina» and Palazzo Massimo alle Colonne), in Bologna and Carpi,

Peruzzi planned Celsi Palace, formerly Pollini, turned the Castle of Belcaro into a villa and carried out the plan for the high altar of the Duomo. The small loggia in the Sanctuary devoted to St. Catherine. Other important 16th-cent. architects were Antonio Maria Lari (reports about him from 1521 to 1549), G.B. Pelori (1488-1558) and above all the painter Bartolomeo Neroni, called «il Riccio» (1500-1573), architect of Tartucci and Chigi alla Postierla Palaces. Between the 16th and 17th centuries, S. Maria di Provenzano, one of the most important churches of Siena, was built (1595-1611), according to a plan of the

1. Torre del Mangia, seen from the open gallery of the Duomo's dome; 2. Fonte Branda and the Basilica of S. Domenico; 3. Façade of the Duomo Nuovo; 4. Antiporto (outside gate) of Camollia; 5. Palazzo Pubblico with Palio flags.

as the highest example of Italian monumental statuary in the early Gothic period. Giovanni Pisano had a great influence on the whole Italian sculpture of the 14th century and the statues of the Apostles, which were once inside the Duomo and are now in the «crypt of the statues», may be attributed to his school. About the Sienese Ramo di Paganello, on the contrary, we do not know almost anything for certain. He was a contemporary of Giovanni Pisano and, when he returned to Siena after the ban imposed on him for adultery, he was called «one of the best and most subtle carvers in the world». Another Sienese, Tino di Camaino, the son of an architect and sculptor is also very famous: he was master builder at the Duomo for several decades. Tino probably began his work in Siena as a pupil of Giovanni Pisano, but later on he abandoned the influence of his master and developed a highly personal style which opposed a powerful sense of mass, gathered inside a quiet, broad and linear outlining, to the bare and vibrating plasticism of Giovanni. Tino di Camaino left in Siena, inside the Duomo, one of his most important works, the tomb of cardinal Petroni (1318). Before that, he had created the mausoleum of Emperor Henry VII of Luxembourg in the Cathedral of Pisa (1315) and later he worked at the Cathedral of Florence; and then in Naples, where he carried out various tombs for the court of the Anjou. Through these last works, Tuscan sculpture spread into southern Italy, where, with the title of First Master, Tino died in 1337. Other significant Sienese sculptors from the 14th century were Gano di Fazio, active in the first twenty years of the century, Agostino di Giovanni and Agnolo di Ventura, celebrated by Vasari for their work in Arezzo, Goro di Gregorio, author of the precious tomb of St. Cerbone in Massa Marittima (1324) and Giovanni d'Agostino, who was able to put the delicate linear elegance of the contemporary Sienese painting into plastic forms. The attribution to Lorenzo Maitani as author of part of the wonderful relief-works on the façade of the Cathedral of Orvieto, on the contrary, is controversial, and most of them are probably to be ascribed to Sienese sculptors, as reported by Pius II in his «Commentari». Maitani was Master Builder at the Cathedral of Orvieto for over twenty years, and he died there in 1330. In the last twenty-five years of the 14th century Giovanni di Cecco, Mariano d'Angiolo Romanelli and others worked at the sculptures of the Chapel of Piazza where a sort of belated revival to the themes of Giovanni Pisano and his circle is to be found. At the beginning of the following century, however, the greatest Sienese sculptor, Jacopo di Piero d'Angelo, called Jacopo della Quercia (1374-1438), became established in Lucca and also in Siena. His style, with the daring power of plastic masses enclosed by fluid contour lines, represents the last and highest expression of the formal Gothic art and, at the same time, belongs to the Renaissance for its new moral responsibility and for the deep humanity which characterizes the allegorical, Biblical and Christian figures as the most genuine prototypes of that austere and dramatic generation of heroes created by the genius of Michelangelo. Among the greatest works of Jacopo is the bas-relief decoration of the main portal of San Petronio in Bologna: in Siena he carried out the remarkable Fonte Gaia on the Campo (1409-1419), worked at the Baptismal Font of S. Giovanni and was Operaio del Duomo (Builder of the Cathedral) until his death. The delicate and elegant artist, Francesco di Valdambrino, was a collaborator of Jacopo, although he showed a completely different nature. He was active from 1401 until about 1430 and carved beautiful wooden statues: a celebrated wood-carver was also Domenico di Niccolò (1363-after 1450), also called «del Coro» or «dei Cori» after the wooden choir he carved and inlaid for the internal chapel of Palazzo Pubblico (1415-28). The Baptismal Font of S. Giovanni, finished by the third decade of the 15th century, represents, with its mirrors of golden brass and its precious small statues, an admirable anthology of the best works produced by Tuscan sculpture in the early Renaissance: here, in fact, can be seen works by the already mentioned Jacopo della Quercia, by Lorenzo Ghiberti and Donatello, who was to work later at the Duomo of Siena. Also minor local craftsmen took part in the building of the font: they were mostly goldsmiths, like Goro di ser Neroccio, Turino di Sano and his son Giovanni di Turino. Later on Antonio Federighi (active from 1439 to 1490) was the most important representative of a Sienese current of elegant and learned Classicism in sculpture, while Lorenzo di Pietro, also called Vecchietta (1410-1480) was showing how deeply Donatello's art had taken roots in Siena. Typical of Donatello is the vibrating pictorialness of the bronze works by Francesco di Giorgio Martini who had as pupils Giacomo Cozzarelli (1455-1515), the author of magnificent groups of polychrome terracotta, and Neroccio di Bartolomeo Landi (1447-1500), better known as a painter. The taste for a decorative sculpture with thin and fine intaglio and rich in Classically-inspired themes, which had spread thanks to Federighi, was continued by the son of Sassetta, Giovanni di Stefano (1443-ca.1504), also the author of remarkable bronze works and of stucco statues, and culminated in the highly elegant virtuosity of Morenzo di

1. Duomo, Crucifixion, from the pulpit by Nicola Pisano; 2. Monument to Cardinal Riccardo Petroni, by Tino di Camaino; 3. Loggia in Palazzo Pubblico: one of the statues originally belonging to the Fonte Gaia, by Jacopo della Quercia.

3

Mariano, also called Marrina (1476-1534). The highest peak of 16th-century sculpture in Siena, however, is represented by the eight bronze Angels bearing candelabra which Domenico Beccafumi (1486-1551), the greatest Sienese painter of that century, modelled for the Duomo in the last years of his life. Sienese sculptors of the late 16th cent. and of the 17th cent., like Fulvio Signorini and Tommaso Redi, are figures of minor importance, but, in the second half of the 17th century, the Cappella del Voto inside the Duomo was to house the wonderful statues of Gian Lorenzo Bernini and those of his pupils Antonio Raggi and Ercole Ferrata. Among Bernini's followers were members of the Mazzuoli family, Dionisio, his sons Giuseppe il Vecchio and Giovanni Antonio, and his grandchild Bartolomeo, who was active until the mid-18th century. During the last century Giovanni Duprè (1817-82) had great prestige and Tito Sarrocchi (1824-1900) and Emilio Gallori (1854-1924) produced works of some value.

Painting

The reason why Siena occupies a rel evant place in art history is that during the Middle Ages it was the seat of a school of painters among the most important in Europe. Two are the currents which stand out among all those of the

14th century, and, for their richness and the vaste scope of themes and expression, they seem to underline and symbolize the figurative possibilities of those days: the Florentine school, focused on Giotto's genius, and the Sienese one, whose greatest figures were Duccio di Boninsegna, Simone Martini, Pietro and Ambrogio Lorenzetti. The two currents, being different as they are in their particular stylistic solutions, also represent two distinct, in some aspects even contrasting, spiritual attitudes. These differences were well understood even by ancient storiographers and today we still accept what a scholar, with a successful intuition, said about it in the 18th century: «Florence seems to me a land of thinkers, and Siena of poets: while the former may produce philosophers, the latter is able to give us bright and imaginative artists». The imaginative and lyric features of Sienese art, which seems almost opposed to the lucid rationality of the Florentine art, which shows, however, highly poetic manifestations, is visible above all in the constant preference of painters for colours and for lines seen as a pure and free expression of a typically decorative sensibility. Florentine artists considered, on the contrary, these two elements as minor aspects in their art works and theirs was rather a research for relief effects in order to confer an almost tangible feature to their representations. So, for example, Giotto's powerful and concise language is opposed to the ethereal and flowered elegance of lines in Simone Martini's work, and the light-and-shade, intensively constructive disposition of mass and volume typical of the Florentine artists is opposed to the quietly chromatic layers of Ambrogio Lorenzetti. Several factors contributed to create the stylistic principles to which the Sienese painters, although with a great variety of results and personal solutions, remained basically true during the whole 15th century. One of the major unifying factors was the persistence of the Byzantine colouristic taste, interpreted in a particularly refined way both by some anonymous miniaturists, to whom we owe, for example, the *Bible of Montalcino* and the *Psalter of Marturi*, and in typically Romanesque paintings like the altar frontal No. 1 in the Picture Gallery, dated 1215, as well as the works which are attributed to the «Maestro di Tressa». And if Guido da Siena, the first painter who can be identified for certain in the Sienese art history, demonstrates, in his imposing «Maestà», formerly in S. Domenico and dated 1221, although it was finished at least half a century later, that he closely kept to the styles produced then in the towns near Siena, especially

in Pisa, two altar frontals now preserved in the Picture Gallery (No. 14 and No. 15), whose style reminiscent of Byzantine miniatures reaches a level of purity and elegance hardly to be equalled, represent the most significant forerunners of the great art of Duccio di Boninsegna (whose activity is reported from 1278 to 1318). In him a genuine linear expression of clearly Gothic origins is added to a chromatic freshness and the rhythm of the Byzantine tradition: his serene vision brings back to life the poetry of Hellenistic naturalism, from which the Byzantine art derives, and transforms it into an intimacy inspired by penetrating accents of humanity. Duccio had a number of pupils and followers who were active until about the mid-14th century, like the restrained Segna di Bonaventura and his son Niccolò di Segna, the highly refined Ugolino di Nerio and, among all the anonymous ones, the Master of Badia a Isola. In Duccio's pictorial language many aspects of the future Sienese painting tradition are already visible. The linear trends of Duccio's work are therefore continued and brought to their highest imaginative level by Simone Martini (ca.1285-Avignon 1344). His loose figures, enclosed by musically winding outlines, reach sometimes an almost ethereal lightness and are similar to pure arabesques, as, for example, in the famous Annunciation of 1333 in the Uffizi Gallery, formerly in the Duomo of Siena. Differently from Duccio who, as far as we know, never painted frescoes, Martini was the first great Sienese master in this technique. The grandiose Maestà of 1315 in Palazzo Pubblico, where it stands opposite to a war scene dominated by Guidoriccio da Fogliano (1329), is the first work which can be attributed to him with certainty. Later on, perhaps from the time of the Maestà, but mostly towards 1324-25, Simone painted a beautifully frescoed cycle of Episodes from the Life of S. Martino in the Basilica of S. Francesco in Assisi. The artist also worked in Naples where he was dubbed knight by King Robert of Anjou in 1317, in Pisa where he painted a beautiful polyptych for the Dominican friars, in Orvieto and finally in Avignon, where he went as a painter of the Papal court towards 1335 and from which his art spread all over Europe, thus setting up the bases for the «International Gothic». A particularly brilliant follower and collaborator of

1. Museum of the Opera del Duomo, front of the «Maestà» by Duccio di Boninsegna (detail); 2. Palazzo Pubblico, Hall of the Mappamondo: Guidoriccio da Fogliano, by Simone Martini (detail); 3. Museum of the Opera del Duomo: Nativity of Our Lady by Pietro Lorenzetti.

1

Martini was his brother-in-law Lippo Memmi, the son of Memmo di Filippuccio, a Sienese painter who had perhaps been brought up in the school of Giotto in Assisi and was later active in San Gimignano: he has also been recently re-evaluated by critics.

The great painting tradition of Duccio and Martini was to be continued without interruptions, although with different results, in the works of the two brothers Pietro and Ambrogio Lorenzetti, who both probably died during the terrible Black Death of 1348. The former, presumably active since 1306, stands out for his lively dramatic nature and, although aware of the lessons of Duccio and Simone, he produced more plastic figures, giving them an intense psychological vitality and an expressive spontaneity, reaching sometimes the highest peaks of drama and tragedy, as can be seen in his greatest fresco, a cycle of Episodes from Christ's Passion, in the lower Basilica of Assisi. Besides these frescoes, and other ones painted in Siena, Pietro also carried out a number of paintings on wood panels which, from the monumental polyptych made in 1320 for the Parish of Arezzo and a Madonna, formerly in the Cathedral of Cortona, to the splendid altar-piece of the Carmine from 1329 and the Virgin's Nativity for the Duomo of Siena in 1335-42, testify of the gradual development in the artist's style, aiming also towards more and more complicated narration schemes and perspective solutions.

The nature of Ambrogio Lorenzetti, on the contrary, must have been completely different from Pietro's. He was probably slightly younger than his brother and his works are reported since

1319: his broad and grandiose style, in fact, shows an interior calm and a state of contemplation which was often compared to eastern spirituality, although representing also a tendency to illustrate the most delicate and intimate feelings. Entirely free from Duccio's influence and aiming, like his brother, at a genuinely Sienese interpretation of the new figurative «vulgar» language of Giotto, Ambrogio was active in Florence probably on different occasions and, besides several painted panels, he left in Siena one of the most famous non-religious painting cycles of the 14th century, the Allegories and the Effects of Good and Bad Government, frescoed from 1337 to 1339 in Palazzo Pubblico, in which a very complicated symbolic concept is rendered by a very high and pure artistic representation. In spite of their different nature and language, the two brothers held for some time a common workshop and painted together in 1335 a cycle of frescoes on the façade of the Spedale church, destroyed in the 18th century, which was taken as example by many painters from the following generations. The mysterious figure of Barna or Berna, on the contrary, lies outside the world of the two Lorenzetti: the Episodes from the New Testament frescoed in the Collegiate church of San Gimignano and datable from a period before the mid-14th century, are in fact related to Duccio's lesson and, above all, to that of Simone Martini and are characterized by a vigorous and immediate expressiveness, marked by an almost popular touch, rich in dramatic accents. It should be noted how recent critics even tend to deny Barna's existence, although Vasari dedicated one of his «Lives» to him, and

they attribute the frescoes of San Gimignano to Lippo Memmi, to his brother Federico (about whom, however, we do not know almost anything), or to a «school of the Memmi». A number of other painters learned indeed very much from the experience of the Lorenzetti and mixed their lesson with different ones: one of them, for example, was given the exegetic name of «Ugolino Lorenzetti» because his manner came from a mixing of what he had learned from Ugolino di Nerio and from Pietro Lorenzetti. Probably, contrary to what many still believe, he was however a different person from the so-called «Maestro di Ovile» who can be identified with Brother Bartolomeo Bulgarini. The most important follower of Pietro Lorenzetti is Lippo Vanni, who had worked as a miniaturist in Siena since 1341, and later as a painter in Naples, and who created his masterpiece in the frescoes portraying the Episodes from the Virgin's life in the church of S. Leonardo al Lago (about 1360-70). During the 14th century, although with a big difference of outcome, several artists produced valuable works: Jacopo di Mino del Pelliccciaio, Niccolò di Bonaccorso, Luca di Tommè, Bartolo di Fredi, Biagio di Goro Ghezzi, Paolo di Giovanni Fei, Andrea Vanni and Andrea di Bartolo. The greatest among them was Taddeo di Bartolo (ca.1362-1422), active between the 14th and the 15th centuries, who worked in Siena, Pisa, Volterra, Perugia and in Liguria contributing to spread, in a nobly academic form, the great tradition of the Lorenzetti brothers; Martino di Bartolomeo, a painter whose activity is reported from 1389 to 1434, shows only a slight influence of that tradition. A significant renewal in the Sienese painting «milieu» was brought about by Stefano di Giovanni, also called «Sassetta», of whom we have information from 1423 to his death in 1450. He interpreted the principles of perspective representation, then beginning to spread in Florence, in a very personal way, although he kept to the slightly unreal Medieval mode of representation. The enamelled brightness of his colours, which cover gentle and slender forms with soft and delicate shades, and the genuinely poetic tone of his narrative works make him an absolute leader over his contemporaries, among whom we can find the so-called «Maestro dell'Osservanza», the author of several wood panel previously attributed to Sassetta, who is characterized by a simpler structure,

1. Art gallery: A seaside town, by Ambrogio Lorenzetti; 2. Municipal Museum: Genuzia being freed from the Devil during the funeral of St. Bernardino, by Neroccio di Bartolomeo Landi.

more typical of the Gothic taste. The very active Sano di Pietro (1406-1481) shares some aspects with this genuine master: in a rich series of precious altarpieces with shining, golden backgrounds, in which he sometimes seems to be repetitive (his workshop was, however, very busy), he was able to express, by means of a high language, still belonging to the Gothic world, the sweetness and the ingenuously devout character of his nature. The artistic career of Giovanni di Paolo (1399-1482), one of the most original painters of the whole Sienese school, ran on a parallel level with that of Sano di Pietro: he was endowed with an unrestrained imaginative sense which brought him to distort reality with extraordinary boldness. In his paintings a fervently lyric feeling is prevailing: lines are sometimes full of tension, sometimes nervous and vibrating while they give objects a bare appearance and almost the signs of physical decay, in some cases bordering on the grotesque. Deeply rooted into the Gothic sense of unreality, and insensitive to external cultural stimuli (apart from the slight influence which Gentile da Fabriano had on him during his stay in Siena in 1425 and 1426), as well as to the changes going on in Sienese painting, Giovanni di Paolo probably spent his long active life without ever leaving his town. Pietro di Giovanni d'Ambrogio (1410-1449) was considered a follower of Sassetta, even if he probably knew Masaccio's and perhaps Paolo Uccello's works, as can be seen in his rigorous portraying of S. Bernardino for which he is mostly famous; and some influence of the art of Masaccio and of the sculpture of Jacopo della Quercia is visible in the first documented works by Domenico di Bartolo (of whom we possess information from 1428 to 1447), datable from the period before the painting of the big cycle of frescoes with episodes from the hospital life, in the Pilgrim ward of the Spedale of S. Maria della Scala. Lorenzo di Pietro, also called «Vecchietta» (1410-1482), already mentioned as a sculptor, was also a talented painter and in his school were brought up artists such as Francesco di Giorgio Martini, a famous architect and sculptor (1439-1501), who shared for some time a workshop with Neroccio di Bartolomeo Landi (1447-1500) whose work, at the dawn of the 16th century and in spite of his up-to-date culture, shows the persistence of a delicate Gothic linear style typical of Simone Martini. Probably the greatest painter of the second half of the 15th century, and certainly the most prolific one in Siena at that time, was Matteo di Giovanni (Borgo S. Sepolcro, ca.1430-died 1495), an artist in whose

eclectic cultural elements of different origins, Sienese as well as Florentine and also from Northern Italy, which had reached Siena through the works of two great miniaturists, Liberale da Verona and Girolamo da Cremona, were merged into an original language. In his work the extraordinary and melancholic sweetness of many Madonnas and the cruel realism in the three works on the Slaughter of the Innocents coexist because they represent different expressions of an extremely sensitive nature and they are rendered by genuine poetry. A close follower of Matteo was Guidoccio Cozzarelli (ca.1450-1517), a modest artist with some degree of gentleness: more significant are the paintings by Benvenuto di Giovanni (1436-1518), in which the clumsiness of crowded scenes is compensated by a clear almost geometrical plasticism of forms, which, however, slackened in the works of his son, Girolamo di Benvenuto (1470-1524). Andrea di Niccolò (ca.1470-after 1514) produced gracious works although of almost rude inspira-

2

tion, supported, however, by a high and diligent skill. By that time, outside elements, having no links with the genuine local tradition had taken root in the Sienese artistic culture. The Sienese activity of Luca Signorelli, of Perugino and of Pinturicchio had a deep influence on the style of several minor painters such as Pietro di Domenico (1267-ca.1533), Bernardino Fungai (1460-1516), the so-called Matteo Balducci and Giacomo Pacchiarotti (1471-after 1539). The works traditionally attributed to Pacchiarotti have been however attributed by recent criticism to the younger Pietro di Francesco Orioli (1458-1496). A significant example of stylistic eclecticism and of the following changes in Sienese painting is given by Girolamo del Pacchia (1477-after 1537), who went from the above mentioned painting styles, typical of Siena and Umbria, to those of the early 16th century in Florence and was later

influenced by Sodoma: he probably died in Fontainebleau. Although he was not Sienese, neither by birth nor by upbringing, Giovanni Antonio Bazzi from Piedmont, also called Sodoma, (Vercelli 1477-Siena 1549), who grew up in his native region and came under the influence of the Milanese followers of Leonardo da Vinci, has a right to artistic citizenship in Siena: both because he was intensively active there and in the area surrounding the town and because his work brought about decisive changes in Sienese painting. In fact, not only did artists like the mediocre Girolamo Magagni, called Giomo del Sodoma, and the more talented Bartolomeo Neroni, called Riccio (a good architect and scene painter) follow his manner, but his work influenced also, for some time, the painting of the great architect Baldassarre Peruzzi (1488-1536), who began as a follower of Pinturicchio and then chose to follow Raphael's example. Also Domenico Beccafumi (1486-1551), undoubtedly the greatest Sienese painter from the 16th century and an imitator of Sodoma, showed of course an open stylistic relation with him: an artist of bright and fervent imagination, a bold colourist and the inventor of complicated and grandiose scenes, he was one of the founders, perhaps the first one, of the great Italian Mannerism. At the end of the 16th century and at the beginning of the 17th century a group of several painters was working in Siena, all showing more or less marked relations to the Manneristic taste: the oldest of them was Arcangelo Salimbeni (died 1580), who had been a pupil of Riccio: his son, Ventura Salimbeni (1568-1613) was a brilliant and elegant painter of frescoes, the greatest in Siena after Beccafumi. Francesco Vanni (1563-1610), half-brother of Ventura, was brought up under the influence of the Roman and Bolognese Mannerists and also of Barocci: a delicate and refined colourist, he is considered the greatest representative of the Counter-Reformation spirit in Sienese painting for the gently and sincerely religious nature of his numerous paintings. Far less significant were his son Raffaello Vanni (1587-1673) and Alessandro Casolani (1552-1606), both influenced by the Roman Mannerism, Sebastiano Folli (1568-1605), the anticipator of a particular provincial Baroque and Pietro Sorri (1556-1621), in whose paintings echoes of the art of Titian and of Veronese appear for the first and last time in Siena. During the 17th century Siena had two very important painters, Rutilio Manetti (1571-1635), who, out of the late Sienese Mannerism of Salimbeni and Vanni, became then one of the most

1

original interpreters of Caravaggio's techniques (his son Domenico is of lesser importance) and Bernardino Mei (1612-1676), who has been greatly re-evaluated by recent criticism, and whose pathetic painting is now seen as a style markedly close to the Baroque naturalism of Mattia Preti, the great «Cavalier Calabrese» who worked in Siena on different occasions. Other painters from the 17th century were Astolfo Petrazzi (1580-1653), the founder of a painting Academy, Francesco Rustici, also called Rustichino (1580-1626), celebrated for his «candlelight» paintings, Stefano Volpi (1585-1642), Niccolò Tornioli (1598-Rome 1652), Deifebo Burbarini (1619-1680), G.B. Ramacciotti (1628-1671) and Francesco Nasini (1621-1695), native of Casteldipiano on the Mount Amiata and founder of a family of painters, the most famous of whom, and much celebrated in his own time, was Giuseppe Nicola Nasini (1657-1736): they were active above all as fresco painters in Siena and in several churches in the surrounding countryside. In the 19th century the fresco tradition was also continued at a particularly high level in Siena, through the works of the brothers Alessandro and Cesare Maffei

first, and then through Amos Cassioli (1832-1892), Cesare Maccari (1840 - Rome 1919), Pietro Aldi (1852-1888) and Alessandro Franchi from Prato, who, after succeeding to Luigi Mussini as director of the local Fine Arts Academy, became with him the representative of the puristic current which shaped a considerable part of the Sienese art of the last century. Other significant Sienese painters from that century were Angiolo Visconti (1829-1861), Gaetano Marinelli (1828-1924) and Ricciardo Meacci (1856-after 1916), and, in our century, Arturo Viligiardi (1869-1936) and Dario Neri (1895-1958).

Other Arts

Other art forms which were widely practised in Siena, and which created masterpieces of quality and importance comparable to those of painting and sculpture, do not deserve the denomination of «minor» arts. The wonderful floor of the Duomo, for example, something unique in its kind, was made with the inlay technique over a period of two centuries, and its stories and symbolic scenes were drawn by great painters and sculptors (Matteo di Giovanni, Pinturicchio, Neroccio di Bartolomeo, Domenico di Bartolo, Urbano da Cortona, Benvenuto di Giovanni, Beccafumi and others). The floor's final stone arrangement was then masterly *levelled* by very skilful hands. During the 14th century Sienese goldsmith's art ranked first in Italy: for example, the much celebrated reliquiary of SS. Corporale in Orvieto was made by a Sienese craftsman, Ugoli-

no di Vieri, and in that century not only did Sienese goldsmiths work in many Italian centres, but they also were called to the most important European courts, to Avignon, to Hungary, to Spain and even to England. Transparent enamel, that is coloured and transparent glass paste covering niello-figured silver plates, was invented by Sienese goldsmiths towards the end of the 13th century. This art, which in the 14th century made famous the names of Guccio di Mannaia, Ugolino di Vieri, Viva di Lando, Toro di Petruccio, Giovanni di Bartolo and Bartolomeo di Tommè, was continued in the 15th century by Francesco d'Antonio, Goro di ser Neroccio and in several anonymous works, all of them being characterized by the most refined elegance. Also the art of stained-glass windows had in Siena one of the oldest and most famous example, namely in the circular «eye» of the Duomo, finished in 1288 and made according to the cartoons by Duccio di Boninsegna. As for miniature painting, it was practised by almost all the painters of the 14th and 15th centuries, but particularly significant were those by Niccolò di ser Sozzo di Stefano and Lippo Vanni, while in the 15th century, besides the books illuminated by Sano di Pietro, Giovanni di Paolo, Guidoccio Cozzarelli and others in the Libreria Piccolomini, appeared the illuminated choir-books by Liberale da Verona and Girolamo da Cremona, which represent the highest achievement of Italy's Renaissance miniature painting. Siena had also very good artists in ceramics, the Mazzaburroni family, while the rich local production of wrought-iron works, textiles and embroideries testifies of the wonderful accomplishment and harmony which the town of Siena reached in every artistic field.

1. Duomo, Piccolomini Library: Enea Silvio Piccolomini being elected Pope with the name of Pius II, fresco by Pinturicchio; 2. Art gallery, Fall of the rebel Angels, by Domenico Beccafumi; 3. Piazza del Campo and Torre del Mangia seen from the Duomo Nuovo. On pages 20-21 aerial view of the town.

2

The centre of the town's life is the CROCE DEL TRAVAGLIO where the three main streets of Siena converge, that is BANCHI DI SOPRA, BANCHI DI SOTTO AND VIA DI CITTÀ, and its name comes from the fact that during the Middle Ages the Sienese used to erect there barricades of beams, «travate», to prevent the enemy's cavalry to come in. The **LOGGIA DEL-LA MERCANZIA**, the Merchant's Loggia, also called LOGGIA DI S. PAOLO or LOGGIA DEI NOBILI, looks over the Croce: it is a beautiful construction with a wide three-arch open gallery by Sano di Matteo (1417-1429). Raised during the 17th century, the Loggia shows, in the ground floor, a transition style from the Gothic to the Renaissance and, inside the tabernacles on the pilasters, statues of *St. Peter* by Vecchietta (1460), of *St. Ansano* and *St. Vittore* by Federighi (1456-63), of *St. Paul* by Vecchietta (1458) and, on the left side, of *St. Savino* by Federighi. Vaults are decorated with stuccoworks and frescoes from the 16th century by Pastorino de' Pastorini (the first one) and by Lorenzo Rustici (the second and the third). In the interior, the shortest sides of the open gallery are closed by two beautiful marble benches with relief figures: on the right bench are the *Famous Romans* by Federighi (1464) and on the left one the *Cardinal Virtues* by Urbano da Cortona (1462). The upper floors of the building house the seats of the Circolo degli Uniti and of the Provincial Tourist Board.

Through the two side-streets which run beside the Loggia or just a bit further through the COSTARELLA DEI BARBIERI, we come down to the **PIAZZA DEL CAMPO** (also called «Campo»), which is slightly concave and shaped of a shell, with its centre paved with bricks (in 1347) and divided into nine «slices» (in memory of the government of the «Nine») by means of travertine stone lines which fan out of the centre. The Campo represents a magnificent example of Medieval town-planning, with its admirable proportions between the wide free space and the series of once embattled buildings overlooking it. In it all Sienese historical events took place, from the triumph for the victory at Montaperti (1260) to the fall of the Republic after the siege in 1555; it heard St. Bernardino and brother Filippo da Lecceto preaching and it saw Provenzano Salvani «tremar per ogni vena» (tremble like a leaf), as Dante wrote in his Divine Comedy (Purgatory, XI, 133-138), after humiliating himself and begging for the ransom a friend of his who had been captured by Charles I of Anjou at Tagliacozzo; it collected assemblies of the people and was a stage for innumerable feasts and tournaments,

Piazza del Campo

Merchant Loggia • Piazza del Campo • Palazzo Pubblico • Torre del Mangia • Cappella di Piazza • Municipal Museum

from the ancient games of «Elmora» and «Pugna» to the race of milk buffalos and the famous «Palio». On the upper part of the paved area is the **Fonte Gaia**, a fountain fed by a water system dating back to 1345: its original marble works, sculptured from 1409 to 1419 by Jacopo della Quercia, corroded and decayed by the ravages of time, were removed in 1868 and replaced by copies made by Tito Sarrocchi. Part of the original sculptures are preserved in the open gallery of the Public Palace. On the southern side of the square we can see the façade of **PALAZZO PUBBLICO** - Public Palace -, the seat of the Municipality and a perfect expression of civil Gothic architecture from Tuscany, whose main body, begun in 1297, was enlarged from 1307 to 1325 with two lateral wings and raised

by one floor in 1680, thus keeping to the style of the existing part. In 1325 the foundation of **Torre del Mangia** were laid (the tower was given this name after a caretaker who was responsible for the striking of the hours, Giovanni di Duccio, nicknamed «il Mangiaguadagni» (the earning-eater) or simply «Mangia», later replaced by an automaton). The brothers Muccio and Francesco di Rinaldo from Perugia, directed by Agostino di Giovanni, worked in 1339 at the building of the tower made of fired bricks, which, with its beautiful belfry of travertine stone (which is traditionally considered as a work planned by the painter Lippo Memmi, although this has never been proved), reached in 1348 the height of 88 mt. The tower's lightning rod goes up to 102 mt. and at its top, inside an

3

iron scaffolding, is a big bell from 1666, popularly called «Sunto», after S. Maria Assunta. In 1354, as a votive offering after the 1348 plague, the **Cappella di Piazza** (Square Chapel) was built at the base of the tower; it was finished in 1376 with Gothic forms by Giovanni di Cecco and, in 1468-70, it was enriched, instead of a porch roof, with a beautiful Renaissance crowning by the sculptor Antonio Federighi: in the niches outside the pilasters are six statues representing the Apostles sculptured from 1377 to 1382 by Mariano d'Agnolo Romanelli and Bartolomeo di Tommè also called «Pizzino» (*St. Jacob the Elder, St. Jacob the Younger, St. John the Evangelist, St. Peter* and *S. Thomas*) as well as by Lando di Stefano, and the panels of the enclosure were carried out in 1848 by Enea Becheroni to replace those of 1470 by Guidoccio Cozzarelli. The wrought iron screen is by Conte di Lello Orlandi and by Orlando di Petruccio (15th cent.).

The façade of the Palace shows a stone ground floor with a series of typical Sienese arches (depressed arches having a falcate ogive on top), while its upper floors are of bricks, with three-light mullioned windows inside lunettes, where, as precious enamels, the black and white symbols of the town (the «Balzana») are displayed. The big copper disk with Christ's monogram was placed there in 1425 in memory of the preaching of St. Bernardino. Through a door in the right wing we come into the offices of the Town Hall, which are arranged around a wide vestibule: inside it, two *gargoyles in form of she-wolves* by the school of Giovanni Pisano, and, on the right wall of the third bay, *St. Peter Alexandrine*

and the *Blessed Ambrogio Sansedoni* and *Andrea Gallerani* by Sano di Pietro (15th cent.) can be seen. In the Anteroom of the Mayor, also called «room of Biccherna», on the left is a big *Crowning of the Virgin with St. Bernardino and St. Catherine*, frescoed by Sano di Pietro in 1445 over an earlier Crowning by Lippo Vanni, and, on the vault, other 17th-century frescoes. Further on, there are rooms frescoed by Vecchietta (*Our Lady of Mercy*, 1461) and by Sodoma (*Resurrection* and a *Madonna with two Saints*): the first room to the left was once the chapel of the Nine, with 14th-century frescoes.

Two doors next to the Cappella di Piazza lead to the Cortile del Podestà (Courtyard of the Podesta), a gloomy and charming place from which a beautiful partial view of the Tower is offered and where the remains of the statue of «Mangia» (18th cent.) can still be seen. On the back is the entrance to the TEATRO DEI RINNUOVATI, set up inside a massive building erected in 1342, and occupied one by a prison and the hall of the Council: the theatre, built in 1562 by Riccio, was rebuilt in 1753 by Antonio Galli Bibiena.

On the right of the courtyard we come to the entrance to the MUSEO CIVICO (Municipal Museum) and to the Monumental district. Modern flights of stairs lead down to the ancient and suggestive MAGAZZINI DEL SALE (salt storehouse), adapted in 1979 to be used as halls for temporary exhibitions. Near the entrance is a 15th-century marble *She-wolf* with twins, the symbol of Siena, originally on the column of Postierla Square: on the upper landing we can see

some Sienese ceramics made during the 17th and 18th centuries. Then the visit continues to the PICTURE GALLERY: ROOM 1 - Non-Sienese and non-Italian painting from the 16th, 17th and 18th centuries; among the exhibited works the *Samaritan at the well* by Mattia Preti and a nice old copy of *Tobiah healing his blind father* by Bernardo Strozzi. ROOM 2 - Sienese painting from the 16th and 17th centuries; let us mention the sinopite and the remains of a big fresco with the *Virgin and the four lawyer Saints of Siena* by Sodoma (1539), formerly in the Cappella di Piazza, as well as wood paintings and canvases by Riccio, by Alessandro Casolani, Vincenzo Rustici and Ventura Salimbeni. ROOM 3 - Sienese Painting from the 16th and 17th centuries; particularly interesting for its representation of the ancient layout of Piazza del Duomo (Cathedral square) is a *Procession* by Agostino Marcucci and canvases by Sebastiano Folli and Astolfo Petrazzi: in the middle of the room there is a big French *Globe* from the 18th century. ROOM 4 - Sienese painting from the 17th and 18th centuries; among these paintings are a banner by Sebastiano Folli, a *St. Paul* and an *Adoration of the Magi* by Rutilio Manetti (1625) as well as canvases by Domenico Manetti, Astolfo Petrazzi, Bernardino Mei, Giovanni Paolo Pisani, Apollonio, Francesco, and Giuseppe Nicola Nasini and by others. In the glass case are examples of Sienese goldsmith's art from the 16th to the 19th century.

Through a short corridor we come to the ROOM OF THE RISORGIMENTO, once part of the Podesta's apartment and devoted to the deeds of Victor Emmanuel II, King of Italy, under whose rule Italy was unified. The paintings on the ceiling and on the walls document a fresco painting tradition which was still alive in Siena during the last century. On the vault, with decorative partitions by Giorgio Bandini, the *Allegory of unified Italy* by Alessandro Franchi (1887) and, in the pendentives, the *Regions of Italy* by Alessandro Franchi, Ricciardo Meacci, Gaetano Marinelli and Antonio Ridolfi. On the walls is *Victor Emmanuel meeting Marshal Radetzky after the battle of Novara* by Pietro Aldi (1886), the *Battle of Palestro* and the *Battle of S. Martino* by Amos Cassioli (1886): these are the best scenes of the whole cycle, the *Meeting with Garibaldi at Teano* by Pietro Aldi (1886), the *Presentation of the plebiscite to Victor Emmanuel II* by Cesare Maccari (1886) and the *Funeral of Vic-*

1. 2. Merchant Loggia: outside and arcade vaults; 3. Piazza del Campo; 4. Piazza del Campo seen from the Torre del Mangia.

3

tor Emmanuel II by the same author (1887). A beautiful walnut cabinet carved by Pietro Giusti contains the uniform worn by Victor Emmanuel II at S. Martino (24 June 1859) and another one, the uniform of Luciano Raveggi, a Major in Garibaldi's army, called the Thousand. A big marble statue representing *Grief* is a work by Emilio Gallori for the tomb of Sienese artists; the busts of *Cavour* and of famous Sienese people are by Giovanni Duprè, Tito Sarrocchi, Enea Becheroni, Giovanni Magi and Arnoldo Prunai, all of them Sienese sculptors from the last century, who, among other works, also sculptured *Flora* and *Charity* (by Tito Sarrocchi) and *Luisa Mussini recumbent* (by Giovanni Duprè). On the panels are some 19th-century paintings of minor importance.

From the adjoining corridor, where five tapestries made in the Medici court in the 16th century are exhibited, we climb up a staircase showing, on its right side, a fresco representing the *Madonna with Child* by Neroccio di Bartolomeo and Mariotto da Volterra (1485) and where, on the first landing, is the door of the gallery of plaster casts exhibiting casts of works by Jacopo della Quercia

4

and some original plaster works by the Sienese Patrizio Fracassi (1875-1903). On top of the stairs we enter a LOGGIA containing the original remains of the FONTE GAIA, formerly on the Campo and sculptured from 1409 to 1419 by Jacopo

della Quercia: although very corroded, these pieces are still wondrous for their plastic power and harmony of lines, showing how Jacopo was able to infuse a new spirit into a language whose stylistic nature was still basically Gothic. The

tion, *Acca Laurentia* and *Rhea Silva*, now interpreted as *Liberality* and *Charity* (the latter presumably carried out with the collaboration of Francesco di Vandambrino). Adjoining the Loggia and behind the stained-glass window is the Sala del Consiglio (Hall of the Council), with 16 vaulting ebbs and as many lunettes, frescoed at the end of the 16th century and at the beginning of the 17th century by various Sienese artists and representing *Episodes of the Town's history*. On the walls are two beautiful canvases by Amos Cassioli: *Provenzano Salvani begging on the Campo to ransom a friend from imprisonment* (1873) and the *Oath of Pontida* (1864). In the adjacent rooms, with lunettes frescoed in the 17th century, is a good collection of coins, prints, maps and models of the town.

While going back down the stairs, on the left we come to the entrance to the SALA DI BALIA with a wooden bench by Barna di Turino (1410) and a «box-seat» with 15th-century inlays. On the vaults are the 16 *Virtues*, frescoed by Martino di Bartolomeo (1408) and on the walls is a cycle of frescoes painted by Spinello Aretino with the help of his son Parri Spinelli (1406-08) and representing the deeds of Alexander III, the Sienese Rolando Bandinelli who was Pope from 1159 to 1181. The cycle, painted on two orders, is divided in two parts: the first, in the second bay for those coming from the corridor, shows the accession to power of Alexander and the struggles he had to fight, while the second, in the first bay, celebrates the generosity and the deeds of the Pope. It begins at the central arch, on the side looking onto the entrance to the «Consistory», with the *22 Cardinals paying their respects to the Pope after deciding, in Ninfa, the election of Rolando Bandinelli* (1159), next to it is the *Appointment in Farfa of Cardinal Ottaviano di Monticello as antipope with the name of Vittore IV* (10 February 1160). Then, on the next wall we can see the *Alexander III crowned Pope in Ninfa* (20 September 1159) and then, above the left window, *Alexander in Anagni receiving a messenger of Barbarossa who tells him that he is not recognized as a legitimate pope* (of uncertain identification). On the end wall, on the left, is *Alexander meets Louis VII King of France in Beauvais* (July 1160) and *Alexander escaping from Rome dressed up as a friar during the town's invasion by Barbarossa* (1167). Back to the wall in front of the window and below the Pope's crowning, is *Alexander*

Fountain, which was named «gaia» (merry) because of the cheerfulness it originated in 1343, when water was finally brought to the Campo, was formed by a rectangular, open-air basin enclosed on three sides by a marble enclosure showing in its middle a bas-relief representing the Virgin with Child and two Angels, flanked by the eight Virtues (particularly beautiful is *Wisdom*, on the left short side): at the ends of the short sides are *the Creation of Adam* and the *Driving away from Eden* and, above, two statues (which were not made in the copy by Sarrocchi, placed in the Campo in 1868), representing, according to tradi-

1. Sansedoni Palace; 2. Fonte Gaia; 3. Detail of the fountain; 4. Palazzo Pubblico.

handing the sword to the Venetian doge *Ziani* followed by the large *Naval battle of the Venetian against the imperial troops at Punta Salvore*. In the first bay, in front of the Battle, is the *The Pope returning to Rome in a procession* (August 1177) and, above, the *Congress of Vienna* (1177, of uncertain identification) and the *Canonization of St. Canuto King of Denmark and of St. Thomas of Canterbury* (1173). Above the window is the *Pardon of Barbarossa* and, above the arch, the *Stake of the 4 antipopes* (Vittore IV, Pasquale II, Callisto IV and Innocenzo III: the episode, however, is apocryphal) and the *Third Lateran synod* (1179). On the wall in front of the window is the *Building of Alessandria*, thus called by the Lombard League in honour of Pope Alexander, and, below, *Barbarossa humiliating himself before the Pope* (1177: the prone figure of Barbarossa was erased for political reasons and later repainted).

We come now into the room of the ANTE-CONSISTORY: above the door are fresco fragments of a «Maestà» with *St. Catherine of Alexandria, St. John the Evangelist* and *St. Augustine with a believer* (the Madonna and the three saints which were once on the left are now missing), attributed to Ambrogio Lorenzetti and below are two wooden statues of *St. Ambrogio* and *St. Anthony Abbot* attributed to Jacopo della Quercia, to whom also the polychrome wooden statue of *St. Nicholas of Bari* is ascribed. The big wooden *Crucifix* is by the 14th-century Sienese school, and the panel representing the *Madonna with Child and 4 Angels* is attributed to Guidoccio Cozzarelli (15th century). On the remaining walls are votive frescoes from the 14th and 15th centuries and, inside the glass case, coffers, small wooden ballot boxes and other objects from the 15th, 16th and 17th centuries, among which is a rich coffer, carved by Antonio Barili (end of the 15th cent.).

HALL OF THE CONSISTORY - The frescoes on the ceiling, with bright colours and daring structure, are among the best works by Domenico Beccafumi (1529-35) and represent famous examples of love for the motherland in Greek and Roman history taken by Valerio Massimo. In the middle of the vault, inside a tondo, *Justice* is represented in a very bold «sotto in su» - upside down -, and, inside two octagons, are *Love for the motherland* and *Mutual Benevolence*. Around the vault, turning left from the entrance, are: *Codro's sacrifice - The tribune Publius Mutius orders his colleagues to be burned - M. Manlius Capitolinus thrown down from the Tarpeian rock - Dictator Postumius sentencing his son to death - M. Emilius Lepidus and Flavius Flaccus become allies again for the sake of the country - The execution of Spurius Melius - The beheading of Spurius Cassius* and *Seleucus of Locri ordering one eye of his son and one of his to be scratched out*. On the walls are three big Gobelins tapestries (17th century), with allegories of the *Earth*, of *Air* and *Fire*, and five smaller Florentine ones (16th century): the marble door is by Bernardo Rossellino and above it is a canvas representing *Solomon's judgement* attributed to Luca Giordano (17th century).

VESTIBULE - Its walls were frescoed in 1871-72 with themes from the 14th century. Above the door is a *Madonna with Child*, a fresco detached from the Loggia, by Ambrogio Lorenzetti (1340) and, between the two doors, a *Sienese she-*

wolf of gilded bronze by Giovanni Turino (1429-30), coming from a column placed beside the door of the palace.

ANTE-CHAPEL - The walls of this room were frescoed in 1414 by Taddeo di Bartolo who represented there four Virtues in the lunettes (*Strength - Prudence - Justice - Generosity*), six whole-length figures and sixteen busts of *Famous men in Roman history* and a huge *St. Christopher*: above the entrance door to the hall of the Mappamondo (the Globe) is *Religion*, on the intrados a map of *Rome*, surrounded by four *Roman deities* and, in the splays, are *Caesar and Pompeius* and *Aristotle*; on the entrance

archway to the chapel are *Judas Maccabeus* and the *Blessed Ambrogio Sansedoni*. Near the door of the Ante-Consistory are two wooden panels representing *Justice* and the *Virgin Mary entrusting Siena to its Podesta* inlaid by Mattia di Nanni also called « Barnacchino» (1425-30). Inside a glass case of precious gold objects, among which is a *Gold rose* by the Pope's goldsmith Simone di Giovanni Ghini of Florence, a gift of Pius II made in 1459 to the Seigniory of Siena, we can admire also a *Peace* of embossed copper and enamels with Christ the Judge and the Four Evangelists, a work by a Sienese goldsmith

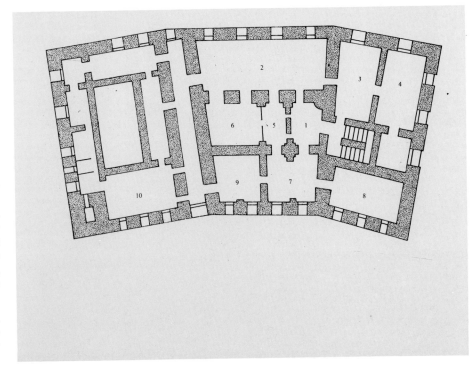

1. The Torre del Mangia seen from Vicolo del Bargello; 2. The Torre del Mangia seen from the courtyard of the Podestà; 3. Cappella di Piazza; 4. Palazzo Pubblico: Room of the Risorgimento.

from the early 15th century, a copper reliquiary for the Head of St. Catherine, from the late 14th century, a circular plate representing the Sienese She-wolf and insignia by Giovanni di Turino and a processional 12th-century Crucifix, from the Meuse region. A bronze holy-water stoup by Giovanni di Turino (1438) stands to the right of the entrance arch to the CAPPELLA DI PALAZZO - the Palace Chapel -, closed by a beautiful wrought-iron gate, carried out according to a plan attributed to Jacopo della Quercia: the walls of the chapel were frescoed in 1407 by Taddeo di Bartolo who represented there the *Annunciation* and the *Last events in the Virgin's life*. Below these works is a series of admirable stalls, whose backs were carved and inlaid with *Articles of the Faith* (1415-1428) by Domenico di Niccolò, later called Domenico dei Cori, to whom has been also attributed a wooden chandelier of rare beauty hanging from the ceiling. The altar-piece representing the *Holy Family with St. Leonard*, comes from the Duomo and is one of the most celebrated works by Sodoma (ca.1533-36). The small, still functioning organ, is by Giovanni Piffero of Siena (1519) and has intaglio works by Giovanni di Pietro and Ghino d'Antonio (1524).

ROOM OF THE MAPPAMONDO (world map) - The room was given this name after a big, circular map on parchment by Ambrogio Lorenzetti (1345), destroyed during the 18th century. The Republican Council used to gather here before the construction of a big building, now occupied by the Teatro dei Rinnuovati. On the end wall the famous «*Maestà*» frescoed in 1315 by Simone Martini is displayed: the fresco was repainted in 1321 by Simone himself because many figures, including the faces of the Virgin and Child, had been damaged by dampness. It is a grandiose painting, which has been, and still is, greatly admired for the delicacy of its chromatic harmony, for the musical purity of its lines and the sweetness of expression of the figures gathered round a very gentle image of the Virgin with Child. The Madonna is sitting on a rich throne, decorated in true Gothic style: two Angels on their knees are offering her goblets full of flowers and behind them are the four Patron Saints of Siena (Ansano, Savino, Crescenzio and Vittore), also on their knees. Twenty-four figures of Saints and Angels are standing, crowding together

Municipal Museum, Sala di Balìa: 1. Comprehensive view with frescoes by Spinello Aretino; 2. Return to Rome of Alexander III; 3. Crowning of Alexander III and handing over of the Sword to the Doge of Venice; 4. Alexander coming back to Rome (detail).

at both sides of the throne, under an ornamented silk pavilion, supported by thin poles, and the whole scene is enclosed by a frame showing twenty medallions with busts of Christ, the four Evangelists, the four Doctors of the Church, the Prophets and the Allegory of the Old and the New Testament. The civic meaning of the painting is explained by two strophes written in beautiful verses, in the style of Dante, under the Virgin's throne: in them she speaks to the Angels and Saints and warns them that, if the powerful were to prevail over the weak or if someone were to betray Siena (PER QUALUNQUE LA MIA TERRA INGANNI), their flower offering and their prayers would not be enough. The fresco's meaning is further explained by a Latin writing on a parchment scroll in the hands of Infant Jesus: DILIGITE JUSTITIAM QUI JUDICATIS TERRAM. This is the first known masterpiece of the outstanding painter who, several years later, when portraying on the opposite wall condottiere *Guidoriccio da Fogliano* riding alone among crete (clay formations typical of Sienese landscapes) and the siege camp of Montemassi (1428), did not alter the tone of his rapt and meditative inspiration, in spite of the thoroughly different theme, thus reaching a very high level of fantastic transfiguration. In 1980 a beautiful fresco representing the *Consignment of a castle* was discovered under the portrait of Guidoriccio, and it is now attributed either to Duccio di Boninsegna or Simone Martini, Pietro Lorenzetti or Memmo di Filippuccio (although this last one, a remarkable painter and the father-in-law of Simone Martini, seems to be the most probable author).

HALL OF THE NINE (also called Hall of Peace, after the most famous figure frescoed on its walls). A wide cycle of frescoes by Ambrogio Lorenzetti (1338) representing the *Allegories and Effects of Good and Bad Government* is displayed on three walls. The complexity of the doctrinal and symbolic content of these frescoes, which comes from Aristotle, is rendered by means of a deep iconographical clarity, thereby becoming a form of pure art and poetic evocation thanks to the harmonious and animated arrangement of the three scenes and to the immediacy of the descriptions of Sienese life, particularly true to the town appearance and the customs of those days. On the wall opposite to the window, the Allegory of Good Government forms the centre of the cycle: on the left is Justice, the foundation of good ruling, looking at Wisdom, placed above; two ropes hang from a pair of scales: on the left pan an Angel, representing Distribu-

3

tive Justice, is beheading a guilty person and awarding a virtuous one, the Angel on the right pan, representing Commutative Justice, is lavishing wealth and power. The ropes are received downwards by Concord, holding on her knees a plane which symbolizes equality among citizens and forms a guide-line for the Twenty-four Magistrates proceeding in a procession headed towards the Commune of Siena, or «Bene Comune» (common good), a «veglio» (old man) dressed in white and black, the colours of the «Balzana», the Sienese she-wolf with the twins at her feet, and, above, the three theological Virtues. Sitting beside the «veglio» are the four cardinal Virtues, Generosity and Peace, a beautiful, languidly lying figure with blond hair intertwined with garlands of olive branches; shields lay at her feet.

Municipal Museum: 1. Hall of the Consistory, vault frescoed with heroic deeds drawn from Roman and Greek history, by Domenico Beccafumi; 2. The Triumph of the Earth, Gobelin tapestry (17th cent.); 3. Comprehensive view of the Chapel; 4. Chapel, fresco by Taddeo di Bartolo.

4

The town is separated from the country-side by walls where an embattled gateway with barbican opens up, through which a group of mounted hunters is coming; beyond the gate is the country-side, a wide landscape of fields, vine-yards, woods and typical Sienese «crete» (clay formations) dotted with working peasants and hunters, while «Securitas» is watching over, warning evil-doers with gallows and a hanged man. On the opposite wall is the *Allegory of Bad Government*, which is embodied by Tyranny, a devil-like being at whose sides are, on the left, Cruelty, Deceit and Fraud, and, on the right, Rage, Discord and War; Greed, Pride and Vainglory are circling around his head, while Despised Justice is lying at his feet with broken scales. The town and the countryside form a desolate picture, with delapidat-ed buildings, heaps of stones and scenes of violence: to the hunters of the previous scene, coming out of a town gate, corresponds a group of people leading a condemned person to his death. On the window wall are false architectural elements by Pietro degli Orioli (1491).

HALL OF THE PILASTERS - It contains paintings on wood panels from the 13th to 15th centuries. Among them is a big *Madonna with Child*, called «Maestà», previously in S. Domenico's, by Guido da Siena and dated 1221: the painting, however, is about half a century more recent and the date 1221 relates probably to an older panel representing the Virgin, whose cult was gradually replaced by the recent one. The heads of the Virgin and Child were restored in the early 14th century by Duccio or one of his close followers. The work, in Byzantine style, is of fundamental importance, both because of its size and because it is the first signed by the painter from Siena who was probably the greatest in his century. Other paintings of the room are: a *Crucifix* attributed to Massarello di Gilio (early 14th cent.), three portions of a polyptych by Martino di Bartolomeo (early 15th cent.), an *Annunciation* (14th cent.), a *Crucifix* by Sano di Pietro and two beautiful parts of a predella representing *St. Bernardino preaching in Siena on the Campo* and the *Saint free-*

Municipal Museum: 1. Chapel. Frescoes with episodes from Our Lady's life: the Apostles' leave and the Funeral, by Taddeo di Bartolo; 2. 3. Inlaid works in the Choir; 4. Room of the Mappamondo. The big Maestà by Simone Martini. Internal pages: Guidoriccio da Fogliano by Simone Martini; on page 39 Hall of Peace. Detail of the frescoes representing Good Government in the town, by Ambrogio Lorenzetti.

1

2

3

ing a possessed woman, by Neroccio di Bartolomeo (second half of the 15th cent.). Then there are two coffers, one of which is preciously gilded with plaster reliefs and images of the Patron Saints of Siena, painted in the early 15th century, and a small stained-glass window representing the *Archangel Michael*, from a drawing attributed to Ambrogio Lorenzetti.

Back to the piazza del Campo, it is possible to admire the beautiful palaces enclosing it in a semicircle: let us mention here the red mass of 14th century SANSEDONI PALACE, with its characteristic rhombus-planned tower, standing out among the others; finally, on the left, the embattled *Elci Palace*.

Municipal Museum: 1. Hall of Peace. Allegory of Good Government; 2. The Effects of Good Government in the countryside; 3. Allegory and Effects of Bad Government, frescoes by Ambrogio Lorenzetti; 4. Hall of the pilasters. St. Bernardino preaching on Piazza del Campo, by Neroccio di Bartolomeo Landi.

4

Coming from the Croce del Travaglio we go up along via di Città, flanked by austere palaces; on our left is the wide, curved façade of 13th-century *Chigi Saracini Palace* (formerly Marescotti Palace), made of stone and bricks, which was enlarged in the late 18th century, and, beside it, a massive 13-century tower. In the courtyard is an open gallery from the 15th century with ground floor vaults painted with grotesques by Giorgio di Giovanni (16th cent.). The palace is the seat of the Accademia Musicale Chigiana, founded in 1939 by count Guido Chigi Saracini as a specialization school for composers. The interior was restructured towards 1922 by Arturo Viligiardi who turned a former dancehall into a concert hall in 18th-century style: on its ceiling is a fresco by Viligiardi himself, representing the *Return from the battle of Montaperti*. In the adjoining rooms and on the upper floor is the most beautiful Sienese private collection (now belonging to the Monte

Piazza del Duomo

The Crypt of statues • The Baptistery • The Museum of the Opera del Duomo • Archiepiscopal Palace • Church and Spedale of S. M. della Scala

dei Paschi, an important bank) with a number of paintings from the 13th and 14th centuries by Sassetta, by Maestro dell'Osservanza, Sano di Pietro, Botticelli, Matteo di Giovanni, Neroccio di Bartolomeo, Girolamo del Pacchia, Sodoma, Riccio, Beccafumi, Brescianino, Rutilio Manetti, Bernardino Mei and other Sienese masters from the 16th to the 19th century, as well as from other Italian and foreign schools. The building also houses a good collection of ancient musical in-

struments. Further on, to the right, is PICCOLOMINI PALACE, also called Palace of the Women-Popes, built in Florentine Renaissance style for Caterina Piccolomini, the sister of Pius II, after a plan attributed to Bernardo Rossellino (1460-65). Past Piccolomini Palace, at the corner with via del Castoro, is MARSILI PALACE, rebuilt in the mid-15th century (1444) with Gothic forms by Luca di Bartolo da Bagnacavallo. Then we come to Piazza Postierla (called «I Quat-

tro Cantoni», 4 Corners), overlooked by the Romanesque FORTEGUERRI TOWER. On the corner of via del Capitano is CHIGI PALACE ALLA POSTIERLA, built during the second half of the 16th century by Bartolomeo Neroni, also called «Riccio». Turning right into via del Capitano we reach the PALACE OF THE JUSTICE CAPTAIN, from the end of the 13th century, although it was completely rebuilt in Gothic style in 1854 by architect Giulio Rossi. The street leads finally to the Piazza del Duomo.

The building of the **DUOMO**, erected on the area where an ancient Cathedral mentioned in the second half of the 11th century had stood, or just nearby, was probably begun at the end of that century or in the early 12th century, and, according to tradition, the church was consecrated in 1179. Towards the mid-13th century, however, it was almost completely restructured, starting from the dome, most probably after a plan by Nicola Pisano, to the front part, carried out in the 7th-8th decade of that century, while, from 1316 onwards, the choir was prolonged by two bays and the transept enlarged. The church, however enlarged, was still not big enough for the increased population. The Sienese were eager to outdo the Florentine who, in those years, were building the huge church of Santa Maria del Fiore. Then, during the fourth decade of the 14th century, an enormous temple was planned: the part of the Duomo built until that time was to be but a transept for the new one. In 1339, under the direction of the Sienese Lando di Pietro, who worked there, however, only for five months, then of Giovanni d'Agostino, the so-called «Duomo Nuovo» was begun: it was planned to lie perpendicular to the right side of the extant one on which it was to be grafted. Quite soon, however, the bad economic situation of the town after the famous 1348 plague, and, above all, some building errors, induced the Sienese to give up the undertaking, which by then had been carried out up to the longitudinal part, with a nave and two aisles having five bays each. In 1357 the vaults and pillars of the left aisle were demolished, while three bays of the right aisle were closed up in order to set up the house of the Opera del Duomo, now seat of a Museum.

Coming from via del Capitano the façade and the right side of the Duomo appear, with the dome and the bell tower erected in Romanesque style, during the 12th century, on an old tower belonging the Bisdomini family with openings increasing in number as they reach the top and covered with thick, «zebra-arranged», black and white marbles. It is better to go through the piazza between one side of the Duomo and the former royal Palace, now seat of the Prefecture (16th cent.), thus coming to the adjoining Piazza Jacopo della Quercia (formerly dei Manetti), formed by what was to be the interior of the «Duomo Nuovo», whose grandiose arches of the right aisle and the framework of the bewilder-

1. Via di Città; 2. Palazzo Ghigi Saracini; 3. Night view of the Duomo; 4. Panoramic view of the Duomo.

ing high façade, called «facciatone», are now to be seen: the rear-façade is clad with striped black and white marbles, and, in its middle, a high, big window is opened, which is actually a two-storey loggia, having an arch with a decoration of classical lacunars. These massive structures enclose a highly suggestive space, in which the magnificence of the unfinished undertaking can be easily imagined. The side door of the Duomo is opened at the base of the bell tower: its lunette contains a relief tondo of the *Virgin with Child*, by Donatello (the original, now replaced by a cast, is in the

1. The Duomo; 2. 3. 4. Details of architectonic elements of the Duomo.

3

4

Museum), and the bronze door wings are by Vico Consorti (1946). Now we come back to the façade, at which Giovanni Pisano worked from 1285 to 1297: the 13th-century plan, however, carried out on the ground floor, was changed in the early 14th century on the overlying part, and the result is that the different plans fit badly to one another. In fact, the two *olimascoli* flanking the central square, where a very large oculus is opened, rather than being a logic extension of the compound columns standing between the central and the side portals, fall wrongly on their curves. What was aimed at was probably something similar to the façade which was then being erected by Lorenzo Maitani for the Cathedral of Orvieto, which was also a source of inspiration for the tricuspid crowning. This heterogeneity of structures, however, is widely balanced by the chiselled preciousness of marble decorations, by the light-and- shade effects in small loggias and by statues.

The part of the church near the portals is a unique example of Giovanni Pisano's genius as an architect and sculptor: the two columns protruding from the splays of the central portal (temporarily removed before being replaced by casts), refinedly engraved with biblical and allegorical figures, are both his and his workshop's. The architrave with *Episodes from the Virgin's life* is considered the first work by Tino di Camaino (ca. 1300) and the bronze door wings with the *Virgin's glorification* are by Enrico Manfrini (1958). Twelve of the big overlying statues, at level with the impost of the portals' arches and on the secondary fronts of the lateral towers, represent the

Prophets and Philosophers of ancient classical times who, according to the then popular beliefs, foretold Mary's virginal childbirth and the coming of the Redeemer. These masterpieces are the works of Giovanni Pisano, now replaced by copies. Copies are also the statues of the Evangelists and the Four Patron Saints of Siena, by followers of Giovanni Pisano, on the upper levels, as well as the busts of *Christ's Forefathers* and the statue of the *Virgin* of Sienese school from the first decades of the 14th century, around the big, round oculus. The

originals of all these sculptures are in the Museum. The mosaics in the triangular pediments of the crowning were carried out in Venice in 1878, the *Crowning of the Virgin* and the *Nativity* after cartoons by Luigi Mussini, and the *Presentation to the Temple* by Alessandro Franchi.

The interior of the Duomo immediately strikes visitors for the vibrating pictorial and perspective effects of the white and black marble stripes covering its walls and pillars, and also for the solemn succession of these piers, which support round arches. The interior work, which

LEGEND FOR THE PLAN OF THE DUOMO

A - Tomb of Bishop Tommaso Piccolomini
B - Chapel of the Madonna del Voto or Chigi
C - High Altar
D - Sacristy
E - Pulpit
F - Chapel of St. John the Baptist
G - Piccolomini Library

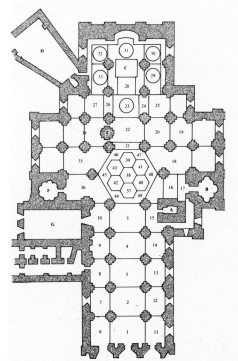

FLOOR LAYOUT

Nave

1. Hermes Trismegistus
2. Coat of Arms of Siena, in the middle, and, around it, of Pisa, Lucca, Florence, Arezzo, Orvieto, Rome, Perugia, Viterbo, Massa, Grosseto, Volterra and Pistoia;
3. Imperial eagle
4. Fortune
5. Fortune and four philosophers

Left aisle

6. The Libyan Sybil
7. The Sybil of Hellespont
8. The Phrygian Sybil
9. The Sybil of Samos
10. The Albunean or Tiburtine Sybil

Right aisle

11. The Delphic Sybil
12. The Cumaean Sybil
13. The Cumanean Sybil
14. The Erythrean Sybil
15. The Persian Sybil

Right transept

16. The seven ages of Man
17. Faith, Hope, Charity and religion
18. The victory of Jefte over the Ammonites
19. Absalom's death
20. Emperor Sigismond on the throne

Presbyterium

21. Moses lets water spring from the rock
22. Adoration of the Golden Calf
23. Psalmist David, David throwing a stone at Goliath already hit
24. Moses
25. The victory of Samson over the Philistines
26. The victory of Joshua over the Amorrines
27. Joshua
28. Abraham's sacrifice
29. Prudence
30. Temperance
31. Mercy
32. Justice
33. Fortitude

Left transept

34. Judith beheading Holofernes and Fighting before the gates of Betullia;
35. The Slaughter of the Innocents;
36. Hercules thrown out of the throne;

Area under the dome

37. Elijah ascending to Heaven;
38. The pact between Elijah and Ahab
39. The sacrifice of Ahab
40. The reproach of Elijah
41. The killing of the false Prophets
42. Ahab's death
43. The sacrifice of Elijah

Inside the rhombuses surrounding the previous panels

44. Elijah raises the Widow's son
45. Elijah anoints Jehu
46. Ardia leads Ahab to Elijah
47. Elijah orders Ardia to bring Ahab to him
48. Elijah fed by deers
49. Elijah asks the Widow for bread

1. Entrance portal of the Duomo Nuovo; 2. Rear-façade of the Duomo; 3. Nave of the Duomo.

shows influences of the two-colour decoration of some Tuscan Romanesque buildings, takes on in the Duomo a particular meaning, probably hinting at the Sienese coat of arms, and contributes, moreover, to enhance the suggestive darkness of the nave and aisles as well as to add to the variety of views created by the connection between the hexagonal supporting pillars of the dome and the bays of the aisles and transept: the whole structure contains so highly scenographic effects as to have led Richard Wagner to use sketches of the interior of the Duomo as a model for the Grail Temple in his Parsifal. The figurative capitals on the pillars are by pupils of the school of Nicola Pisano (Arnolfo di Cambio probably also worked at some of them), and they are datable from 1270; over the arches is a protruding cornice on corbels, among which are 172 heads of Popes (including a bust of Christ over the apse, from which the series begins) dating back to the late 15th century. The nave was raised towards the mid 14th century, and was covered by cross vaults with gilded stars. The interior is 89.52 mt. long, and the decorated floor, stretching for its whole length, is the object of universal admiration. From 1369 to 1546, generations of highly skilful craftsmen worked uninterruptedly at the floor, which was widely restored during the 19th century. They were specialized in turning drawings and cartoons by the greatest artists of their time into marble works using

Duomo: floor. 1. Coat of arms of Siena surrounded by those of the allied towns; 2. Fortune's Wheel; 3. The Erythrean Sybil; 4. Slaughter of the Innocents, by Matteo di Giovanni; 5. Allegory of Virtue Hill, by Pinturicchio.

4

several techniques, from mosaic to inlay, from marquetry to graffito. To each bay of the longitudinal main body corresponds one of the panels, which are arranged as follows: nave: *Hermes Trismegistus*, attributed to Giovanni di Stefano (1488) - *Sienese she-wolf with the symbols of the allied towns*, the only mosaic panel, of unknown author (ca. 1373) and restored during the last century - *Wheel with Imperial Eagle* (14th cent., also restored) - *Allegory of the Hill of Virtue* after a drawing by Pinturicchio (1506) and *Fortune's wheel*, remade after an original from the early 15th century, probably by Domenico di Niccolò dei Cori. In the aisles the ten *Sybils* were carried out between 1482 and 1483: going towards the dome, in the left aisle, we can see the *Libyan* by Guidoccio Cozzarelli, the *Syibil of Hellespont* by Neroccio di Bartolomeo, the *Phrygian* by Benvenuto di Giovanni; the *Syibil of Samos* by Matteo di Giovanni and the *Albunean* by Benvenuto di Giovanni; in the right aisle the *Delphic* by Antonio Federighi, the *Cumaean* and the *Cumanean* by Giovanni di Stefano, the *Erythrean* by Antonio Federighi and the *Persian* by Benvenuto di Giovanni.

On the rear-façade a big oculus is opened, with a stained glass window by Pastorino de' Pastorini representing the

5

Last Supper (1545) and below, on both sides of the portal, are two richly engraved columns made in the workshop of Giovanni di Stefano (1483), formerly on the old altar of the Four Crowned Saints and having on their pedestals reliefs with *Episodes from the Virgin's life* by Urbano da Cortona (1453), formerly belonging to the primitive chapel of the Madonna delle Grazie: the two statues of seated Popes represent, in the right aisle *Paul V* by Fulvio Signorini (1605) and in the left one *Marcellus II* by Domenico Cafaggi (1591). The two splendid holy-water stoups are by Antonio Federighi (ca. 1463). Further on in the right aisle are four altars, restored in the late 16th century, and, up to the lateral entrance, paintings by D.M. Canuti

Duomo: 1. The dome; 2. Holy-water stoup, by Antonio Federighi; 3. Façade's rose-window by Pastorino de Pastorini; 4. The Chapel of the Madonna del Voto with statues representing St. Bernardino, by Raggio, and St. Catherine, by Ferrata; 5. 6. Cappella del Voto: St. Girolamo and Magdalene, by Bernini.

4

5

6

(1681), Annibale Mazzuoli (early 18th cent.), Raffaello Vanni (1654) and by Pier Dandini (1671): beyond the entrance, on the bell tower wall, are the *tomb of Bishop Tommaso Piccolomini del Testa*, by the painter Neroccio di Bartolomeo (1485) and, below, six *Episodes from the Virgin's life* by Urbano da Cortona (1453), formerly in the chapel of the Madonna delle Grazie. Then we pass under the cupola supported by six pillars, on which rest the gilded statues of the *Four Patron Saints of Siena*, of *St. Bernardino* and *St. Catherine* by Giovanni di Stefano (1490): the overlying blind gallery is divided by 42 architraved small columns; between them are 42 monochrome figures of *Patriarchs* and *Prophets* painted by Guidoccio Cozzarelli, Benvenuto di Giovanni and others (ca. 1481). Two flag-poles, thought to have belonged to the Sienese carroccio at the battle of Monteaperti (4 Sept. 1260), stand by the first two pillars. The underlying part of the floor (usually covered), shows seven hexagons with *Episodes from Elijah's life*, four of which were carried out from 1521 to 1524 from cartoons by Domenico Beccafumi, and three in 1878 by Alessandro Franchi. Among the two last pillars is a long strip with *Moses letting water gush forth from the rock* by Beccafumi and, after this, *Moses breaking the Tables of the Law*, by the same author, with remarkable light-and-shade effects similar to those of a paint-

ing. In the right wing of the transept is the CAPPELLA DEL VOTO, an example of the purest Roman Baroque style, built from 1659 to 1663 for Pope Alexander VII (the Sienese Fabio Chigi) after a plan by Gian Lorenzo Bernini in honour of the *Madonna del Voto*, the most revered sacred image of Siena, painted on wood by a follower of Guido da Siena (who has been recently recognized as Diotisalvi di Speme) after the victory of Montaperti (1260) and preserved inside a case supported by two Angels of gilded bronze by Ercole Ferrata. By the walls stand eight columns of green marble coming from S. Giovanni in Laterano and four niches open out on both sides of the en-

Duomo: 1. High Altar with bronze ciborium by Vecchietta and angels bearing candelabra, by Francesco di Giorgio Martini and Giovanni di Stefano; 2. Central part of the choir, after a plan by Riccio; 3. Angel bearing a candelabrum, by Domenico Beccafumi; 4. Bronze tombstone of Bishop Giovanni Pecci, by Donatello (1426).

trance, containing statues of *St. Jerome* and *Magdalene*, among Bernini's masterpieces, and, on both sides of the altar, statues of *St. Catherine of Siena* by Ferrata and of *St. Bernardino* by Antonio Raggi: the overlying reliefs with *Episodes from the Virgin's life* date back to the 18th century, the two big paintings of the *Visitation* and the *Flight into Egypt* are by Carlo Maratta (the latter was made into a mosaic in 1793) and the bronze votive statue representing *Gratitude* in front of the altar is by the Sienese Arturo Viligiardi (1918). We continue our visit in the right transept wing, where, over the altars, are a painting with *St. Crescenzio* by Luigi Mussini (1867) and *St. Bernardino preaching*, one of the masterpieces of Mattia Preti from Calabria, and, in the chapel of the Holy Sacrament, an *Adoration of the shepherds* by the Sienese Alessandro Casolani (1594). On the chapel wall are

reliefs with the *Evangelists and St. Paul*, formerly belonging to a «preaching pulpit», begun by Giovanni di Francesco da Imola and finished by Giovanni di Turino (1426). The two statues of Popes represent, to the right, *Alexander VII* by Antonio Raggi (1663) and, to the left, *Alexander III* by Ercole Ferrata (1667). On the floor are the *Victory of Jefte over the Ammonites* after a drawing attributed to Neroccio di Bartolomeo (1485), *Absalom's death* attributed to Pietro del Minella (1447), and *Emperor Sigismund on his throne* after a drawing by Domenico di Bartolo (1434). Back to the nave, in the middle of the floor is a tondo representing *David composing psalms* and, on its sides, *David with the sling* and *Goliath being struck* after a drawing by Domenico di Nicolò dei Cori (1432), at whose left are the *Story of Joshua* and, on the right, the *Story of Samson*, both probably from a drawing by Sassetta

(1426): further ahead, in front of the high altar, is *Isaac's sacrifice*, wonderfully drawn by Domenico Beccafumi (1546), who shaped also eight beautiful bronze *Angels bearing candelabra* standing by the pillars near the presbytery (1548-51). On the end wall, above, is a big oculus with a stained-glass window divided into nine panels and built in 1288 from cartoons or drawings by Duccio di Boninsegna, the oldest example of wholly Italian production and style in the stained-glass technique. Further below, around and above the apse, in which there is a painting representing the *Assumption* by Bartolomeo Cesi from Bologna (1594), are frescoed *Angels in Glory*, in the bowl-shaped vault, and ten *Apostles*, on their sides, by Domenico Beccafumi, and, at the end of the aisles, the *Fall of Manna*, *Esther and Ahasuerus* and *Sienese Saints and Blessed* by Ventura Salimbeni (1608-11). The under-

lying choir dates back to two different periods: a Gothic one, from the second half of the 14th century, when the two wings were made, into whose backs beautiful mirrors engraved by Giovanni da Verona (1505) were added during the last century, and a pure Renaissance period, when the curved, central part was carried out, between 1567 and 1570, after a drawing by Riccio. On the high altar is a grandiose bronze ciborium by Lorenzo di Pietro, also called «Vecchietta», coming from the church of the Spedale, flanked above by a couple of *candle-bearing Angels* by Giovanni di Stefano, and, below, by two more *Angels*, masterpieces of Francesco di Giorgio Martini (1497-99). The visit continues

Duomo: 1. Chapel of St. John the Baptist; 2. Bronze statue of the Baptist, by Donatello; 3. The pulpit sculptured by Nicola Pisano; 4. Pulpit panel representing Nativity.

in the left transept wing where three big scenes are depicted on the floor: *Story of Judith in Betulia* by Urbano da Cortona, probably after a drawing by Francesco di Giorgio Martini (1473), *Slaughter of the Innocents*, after a drawing by Matteo di Giovanni (1482) and *the Driving away of Herod* by Benvenuto di Giovanni (1485). In the chapel of St. Ansano is the *Tomb of Card. Riccardo Petroni*, one of the most important works of the Sienese Tino di Camaino (1317); on the floor is the *bronze tomb slab of Bishop Giovanni Pecci* by Donatello (1426), and, over the altar, *St. Ansano baptizing the Sienese*, a panel

Duomo: the pulpit. 1. Statue of Our Lady of the Annunciation; 2. Journey and Adoration of the Magi with trilobate small arch; 3. Presentation in the temple and Flight into Egypt; 4. Virgin with Child; 5. Slaughter of the Innocents; 6. The Elect on the Judgement Day.

painting by Francesco Vanni (1596). In the head is the chapel of St. John, where a relic of the Baptist's right arm, donated by Pius II in 1464 is preserved. The chapel, which is closed by a big marble portal, flanked by two columns with pedestals by Antonio Federighi and Giovanni di Stefano (1486), contains an admirable bronze statue of the *Baptist* by Donatello (1457): on the left is a statue of *St. Ansano* by Giovanni di Stefano (1487) and, on the right, a *St. Catherine of Alexandria* by Neroccio di Bartolomeo; in the middle is a small well for the storage of Holy Saturday water by Federighi. Walls were frescoed in 1504-05 by Pinturicchio, who painted there two portraits of *Alberto Aringhieri*, rector of the Opera del Duomo, as a young and as an old man; the *Baptist in the desert* and the *Baptist preaching*: the *Baptist's nativity*, *Christ's baptism* and the *Baptist's beheading* were repainted during the 17th cent. by Rustichino, while the *Baptist imprisoned* is by Cesare Maccari (1868). Near the hexagon of the

dome is the very famous PULPIT, carried out from 1265 to 1268 by Nicola Pisano with the help of his son Giovanni, of Arnolfo di Cambio and others, the oldest and most precious ornament of the whole Duomo. The pulpit, with an octagonal base, is supported at its corners by eight columns alternatively resting on the backs of lions and lionesses, as well as by one more column in the middle, with the *Liberal Arts* and *Philosophy* at its base: these figures bear trefoil arches having at their junctions eight small statues representing the *Virtues* and, in the triangles, groups of two *Prophets*. The overlying gallery has a balustrade formed by seven relief *plutei* (one side is open and gives way to a staircase added in 1543 by Riccio) representing *Episodes from the life of Jesus* and the *Last Judgement*, interrupted at corners by statues and groups of statues in the following order: small statues of the *Annunciation - Visitation, Nativity and Annunciation to the shepherds - Three Apostles - Journey and Adoration of the Magi - Virgin*

with Child (one of the highest achievements of Nicola) - *Presentation to the Temple and Flight into Egypt* (with a probable collaboration of Arnolfo) - First group of *Tuba-playing Angels of Judgement - Slaughter of the Innocents* (probable collaboration of Giovanni) - *Apocalyptic Christ - Crucifixion* (a masterpiece of intense pathos) - *the Elect on the Judgement day* - Group of the *Evangelists* surmounted by a reading-desk bearing the eagle of St. John - *the Elect on the Judgement day - Christ the Judge* and, below, Angels holding the Symbols of the Passion - *the Driving away of the wicked to Hell* - Second group of *Angels of Judgement*. The pulpit, on which 307 persons and human heads and about seventy animals are depicted, represents one of the most memorable events in art history, and Italian sculpture would be influenced by it for over one century.

Through the left aisle we come to the LIBRERIA PICCOLOMINI, with its monumental front engraved by Lorenzo

di Mariano, called «Marrina» (1497) above which is a big fresco with *Pius II's pontifical crowning* by Pinturicchio (1505). The library was founded around 1492 by Card. Francesco Piccolomini Todeschini, later Pope Pius III, to collect there the volumes of the library of his uncle, the great Pope and humanist Pius II (Enea Silvio Piccolomini). It is an airy and bright space in Renaissance style with in its middle the famous group of the *Three Graces*, a good Roman imitation from the 3rd cent., probably from a Greek painting, and with grotesque-decorated vaults and walls frescoed in 1505-07 by Bernardino di Betto, called «Pinturicchio», who represented there,

Duomo: Piccolomini Library. 1. Fresco surmounting the entrance with the Pontifical Crowning of Pius III by Pinturicchio; 2. Marble group of the Three Graces, of the 3rd cent.; 3. Enea Silvio leaves for the Council of Basel; 4. Enea Silvio in front of King James of Scotland; 5. Enea Silvio is crowned poet by Frederick III, frescoes by Pinturicchio.

3

AENEAS SILVIVS PICOLOMINEVS NATVS EST PATRE SILVIO MATRE
CTORIA · XVIII · OCTOB · ANN · MCCCC · V · CORSIANI INFVNE
GENTILITIS BASILEAM AD CONCILIVM CONTENDENS VI TEMPE
TIS IN LYBIAM PROPELLITVR ·

4

AENEAS SILVIVS A BASILIENSI CONCILIO IN VLTERIOREM BRITANNI
AM ORATOR AC SCOTIAM AD REGEM CALEXIVM MISSVS ATEM
PESTATE IN NOVERGIAM PVLSVS ET PER BRITANNIAM REGIOS SPECV
LATORES ELVDENS BASILEAM REVERTITVR·

5

HIC AENEAS AFOELICE · V · ANTIPAPA LEGATVS AD FEDERICVM · III ·
CAESAREM MISSVS LAVREA CORONA DONATVR ET INTER AMICOS
EIVS AC SECRETARIVS ANNVMERATVR ET PRAEFICITVR·

AENEAS A FEDERICO·III·IMP·LEGATVS AD·EVGENIVM·IIII·MISSVS
NON SOLVM EI RECONCILIATVS EST SED HIPPODIACONVS ET SECRETA
RIVS MOX TERGESTINVS DEINDE SENEN·ANTISTES·CREATVS

1

AENEAS FEDERICO·III·IMP·LEONORAM SPONSAM
EXHIBET ET PVELLAE LAVDIS AC REGVAL
LVSITANORVM COMPLECTITVR

2

AENEAS SENEN·ANTISTES AD CALISTVM III·ORATOR AFEDE
RICO IMP·III·MISSVS PONT·AD BELLVM ASIATICVM ARMAT
ET PATRVM PRINCIPVMQ·OMNIVM ROGATIONE·CARD·EFICITVR

3

4

6

5

7

Duomo: Piccolomini Library. 1. Enea Silvio and Pope Eugenio III; 2. Frederick III and Eleonora of Aragon meet near Porta Camollia; 3. Enea Silvio receives the cardinal's hat; 4. Pius II is ordained Pope; 5. Pius II summons the Christian princes for a crusade (detail); 6. Canonization of St. Catherine of Siena; 7. Frescoed ceiling. All frescoes in the Library are by Pinturicchio.

1

2

in full detail and with great freshness of colours, still perfectly preserved, ten *Episodes from the life of Pius II*: 1 - *Enea Silvio, the future Pope Pius II, leaves for the Council of Basle as secretary of Card. Capranica*; 2 - *Enea Silvio says a prayer before King James of Scotland to whom he was sent by the Council of Basle*; 3 - *Enea Silvio is crowned poet by emperor Frederick III*; 4 - *Enea Silvio submits himself to the legitimate Pope Eugene IV*; 5 - *Enea Silvio, Bishop of Siena, having arranged the marriage between emperor Frederick III and Eleonor of Aragon, is present at the meeting of the betrothed in Siena, outside Porta Camollia*; 6 - *Enea Silvio is made a cardinal*; 7 - *Pontifical election of Pius II*; 8 - *Pius II summons Christian princes to Mantua to organize the crusade against the Turks*; 9 - *Canonization of St. Catherine of Siena*; 10 - *Pius II arrives at Ancona to receive the Venetian fleet which was to have taken part in the crusade*. Below the frescoes a series of splendid choir-books is displayed, miniated for the Duomo by Liberale da Verona, Girolamo da Cremona and Sano di Pietro from 1466 to 1475 and by Pellegrino di Marianno, Guidoccio Cozzarelli and Benvenuto Giovanni after 1480.

Back to the left aisle we find the grandiose PICCOLOMINI ALTAR by Andrea Bregno (1481-1503), whose niches contain statues of *St. Peter, St. Paul, St. Pius* and *St. Gregorius*, by Michelangelo (1501-04): *St. Francis*, above, is by Pietro Torrigiano and the small panel painting with the *Madonna of Humility* is by Paolo di Giovanni Fei. Three more altars follow with a canvas by Pietro Sorri and two by Francesco Trevisano.

We can leave the square by passing through the lateral portal of the «Duo-

Duomo: Piccolomini Library. 1. Choir-book miniatures: Nativity by Girolamo da Cremona; 2. Healing of a leper, by Liberale da Verona; 3. 4. 5. Piccolomini Altar with the statues of St. Paolo, St. Gregorio, St. Pietro and St. Pio, sculptured by Michelangelo.

FRAN·PICCOLOM·CAR·SENEN   PII II·PONT·MAX·NEPOS

3

4

5

mo Nuovo» (in whose lunette is a cast of group of statues by Giovanni d'Agostino), beyond which a pictoresque stairway leads down to piazza S. Giovanni. From its first landing we enter the CRYPT OF

1. Portal of the Duomo Nuovo and staircase leading down to the Baptistery; 2. Crypt of the Statues; 3. The Redeemer adored by two angels; 4. The Redeemer, detail of the statue group, by Giovanni d'Agostino, formerly over the portal of the Duomo Nuovo; 5 Façade of the Baptistery; 6. Interior of the Baptistery with Baptismal font.

5

THE STATUES, which is what remains of the late 12th-century crypt of the Duomo, with fragments of frescoes of the school of Guido da Siena (13th cent.), a remarkable marble group with the *Redeemer adored by two Angels*, by Giovanni d'Agostino (ca. 1345), originally from the portal of the «Duomo Nuovo», early 14th-century statues of the *Apostles* and the originals of columns and lions by Giovanni Pisano and his workshop, formerly on both sides of the main portal in the façade of the Duomo.

The façade of the **BAPTISTERY**, built between 1317 and 1325 under the extension of the choir of the Duomo, looks onto the underlying piazza S. Giovanni. Its interior has a nave and two aisles with pointed vaults, whose cells and arch soffit are frescoed with *Articles of the Creed* (1447), *Apostles*, *Prophets* and *Sybils* (1450) by Lorenzo di Pietro, called «Vecchietta», also the author of a *Flagellation of Christ* and an *Ascent to the Calvary* in the apse (1453), on whose bowl-shaped vault is a *Crucifixion*, a *Prayer in the Garden* and a *Mourning over the dead Jesus* by Michele di Matteo da Bologna (1447). Behind the altar is a *Baptism of Christ* by Alessandro Franchi (1908) and, in the big lunettes, to the left, *Three Miracles of St. Anthony of Padua* by Benvenuto di Giovanni (*before* 1466) and, to the right *Washing of the feet* by Pietro degli Orioli (1489). A *baptismal Font* represents a great early Renaissance masterpiece, with reliefs and small statues of gilded brass surrounding the basin, at which the three

6

1

2

3

4

greatest sculptors of those days worked from 1427 to 1430. The reliefs depict the Life of the Baptist with the following arrangement: 1 - *Annunciation to Zacharias* by Jacopo della Quercia; 2 - *Birth of the Baptist* by Turino di Sano and Giovanni di Turino; 3 - *the Baptist preaching* by Giovanni di Turino; 4 - *Christ's baptism* by Lorenzo Ghiberti; 5 - *the Baptist before Herod* by Lorenzo Ghiberti; 6 - *Herod's banquet*, for its Renaissance perspective concept one of the main works of Donatello, also the author of the two beautiful small statues of *Hope* and *Faith*. The marble ciborium rising in the middle of the basin shows five powerful representations of the *Prophets* by Jacopo della Quercia and, on top, a small statue of the *Baptist* by the same author.

Baptistery: 1. An Angel foretells Zacharias the birth of the Baptist, by Jacopo della Quercia; 2. Birth of the Baptist, by Turino di Sano and Giovanni di Turino; 3. The Baptist preaching, by G. di Turino; 4. Christ's Baptism, by Lorenzo Ghiberti; 5. The Baptist before Herod, by L. Ghiberti.   **5**

Baptistery: 1. Herod's banquet, by Donatello; 2. Detail of Herod's banquet; 3. Justice, by G. di Turino; 4. Charity, by the same author; 5. Prudence, also by G. di Turino; 6. Faith, by Donatello.

4   5   6

THE BAPTISMAL FONT

The Baptismal Font, a masterpiece of 15th century sculpture, was carried out in the first half of the 15th century by Pietro del Minnella, Bastiano di Corso and Nanni di Luca for the architectonic parts, while its sculptures are by several other artists.

It is made of a hexagonal basin having in its middle a ciborium, also hexagonal, supported by a pilaster.

On top of the ciborium, planned by Jacopo della Quercia, is a statue of St. John the Baptist, also by Jacopo; among the frontons are four bronze angels, two of whom by Donatello and two by Giovanni di Turino, of 1424; in the niches are five figures of prophets, sculptured by Jacopo della Quercia, and a Madonna with Child by Giovanni di Turino. Around the basin are six bas-reliefs of gilded bronze representing episodes from the Baptist's life, divided by six statues. From left to right, starting from the altar side, are: Zacharias being thrown out of the Temple, by Jacopo della Quercia, of 1417; a statue representing Justice, by Giovanni di Turino, 1424; Birth of the Baptist by Turino di Sano, 1427;

1

2

3

Charity, by Giovanni di Turino, 1424; the Baptist's Preaching, by the same author, 1427; Prudence, also by Giovanni di Turino; Christ's Baptism, by Lorenzo Ghiberti, 1427; Faith, by Donatello; Capture of the Baptist, by Lorenzo Ghiberti, 1427; Hope, by Donatello, 1428; Herod's banquet, by the same author, 1427; Fortitude, by Goro di Neroccio, 1428.

Baptistery: 1. Hope, by Donatello; 2. Fortitude, by Goro di Ser Neroccio; 3. 4. «Flagellation» and «Ascent to Calvary», frescoes by Vecchietta.

4

MUSEUM OF THE OPERA DEL DUOMO

Upstairs the visit continues to the MUSE-UM OF THE OPERA DEL DUOMO, in which sculptures, paintings, pieces of jewelry, miniatures and vestments, coming mostly from the Duomo, are preserved (only the most important works are mentioned here).

GROUND FLOOR - On the left are wooden statues among which is a *St. John the Baptist*, first work of Francesco di Giorgio Martini (1464), then the *hall of sculptures*, divided into two areas by a big 15th-cent. wrought-iron railings resting on marble *plutei* of the school of Nicola Pisano. In the first area to the left, are four Episodes from *Christ's childhood*, from the late 13th cent., the front of a *Roman sarcophagus* with sea deities, a relief representing the *Church and the symbols of the Evangelists* attributed to Lapo, a collaborator of Nicola Pisano, and a tondo with the *Virgin with Child* by Donatello. Beyond the railings, in the middle is a relief with the *Virgin with Child adored by Card. Casini introduced by St. Anthony Abbot*, the last work by Jacopo della Quercia (1438) and, by the pilasters, ten statues sculpted by Giovanni Pisano between 1285 and 1297 for the façade of the Duomo, the most important group of monumental statues in Italian Gothic style, remarkable for the freedom given to each figure's development in space and for their marked individuality, often charged with dramatic tension: to the left, *Moses*, *Mary of Moses*, *Simeon*, a *Sybil* and *Isaiah*, and, to the right, *Solomon*, *Plato*, *Abacuc*, *David* and *Balaam*. Then more statues by Giovanni Pisano and his followers and, above, the *Madonna with Child* and busts of *Christ's forefathers* of Sienese school from the second or third decade of the 14th cent. At the end, inside a 1689 altar, *Christ's baptism*, a panel painting by Andrea and Raffaello Piccinelli, also called «Brescianini» (1524).

Now, going up the stairs, we turn left entering the HALL OF DUCCIO, a temperature-controlled room, where the «Maestà», one of the greatest masterpieces of medieval painting, carried out by Duccio di Boninsegna for the high altar of the Duomo from 1308 to 1311, is preserved. It was originally formed by a big wood panel painted on both sides, detached from one another in 1771. This resulted in the loss of some parts of the predella and of the crowning (eight predella components being now in foreign museums). On the front is displayed a grandiose scene of the *Madonna with blessing Child* surrounded by her celestial court of Saints and Angels, and, in the foreground, the four Patron Saints of Siena (Ansano, Savino, Crescenzio and Vittore) who, on their knees, intercede for the Town: a wonderful vision, shining with gold and warm colours, where the new Western Gothic language is merged with Eastern Byzantine tradition, drawing on its remote Hellenic roots. This is particularly evident in the supreme idealization of the beautiful Angels, who, together with other solemnly and symmetrically arranged figures crowding around the sides of the marble throne, contemplate enraptured the Virgin. On the opposite wall is the back side of the main panel, divided into 26 small pieces depicting Christ's Passion, following those of the predella with Christ's Childhood and Life, displayed on the long side of the hall, together with Christ's Apparitions after Resurrection and Last Episodes of the Virgin's life, which formed once the crowning of the panel. In each episode, rendered with precious clearness in full detail, the Byzantine iconographical patterns seem to be miraculously enlivened by a new and immediate narrating feeling, often transfigured into pure lyrical evocation.

In the same hall: *Madonna with Child*, called «of Crevole», after the place where it was found, a panel painting by the young Duccio (ca. 1283) and *Nativity of the Virgin*, one of the last and highest achievements of Pietro Lorenzetti (1342); in the adjacent rooms, on the right, *Virgin with Child and four Saints*, gilded wooden statues by Jacopo della Quercia and his workshop (ca. 1420-24: three Saints are attributed to Giovanni di Francesco da Imola) and *St. John the Baptist*, also by Della Quercia; in the next room are old architectural drawings, among which are two parchments with plans for the «Duomo Nuovo» and one with a bell tower attributed to Giotto, and 15th-cent. miniated choir-books and documents by artists who worked at the Duomo.

Again on the stairs and turning left, we enter the TREASURE HALL, with in its centre a *Reliquary of St. Galgano's head*, an important work of Sienese goldsmith's art from the late 13th cent., a *Reliquary of a Baptist's arm* by Frances-

Museum of the Opera del Duomo: 1. Hall of sculptures; 2. Virgin with Child, St. Anthony Abbot and Cardinal Casini on his knees, by Jacopo della Quercia; 3. Simeon, detail; 4. Moses; 5. Mary of Moses; 6. Sybil, works by Giovanni Pisano.

2

This work is the altar-piece for the Duomo's high altar, painted from 1308 to 1311, and it represents the highest achievement in Sienese painting, in which Duccio succeeded in wonderfully harmonizing the Byzantine iconographic tradition with a gothic lyricism of French inspiration. The big wooden altar-piece, painted on both sides, was sawn in 1771 after the altar had been removed, to make it easier to observe, and it was moved to the Museum of the Opera in 1878. On its front are represented a Madonna with Child on the throne among angels, the Saints Paul, John the Evangelist, John the Baptist and Peter, the Saints

THE MAESTÀ

BY DUCCIO DI BONINSEGNA
(active between 1278 and 1319)

3

Catherine of Alexandria and Agnese and
the four Patron Saints of the town, Ansano, Savino, Crescenzio and Vittore;
above are the half-busts of ten Apostles.
At the foot of the throne is a Latin inscription meaning: «Holy Mother of
God, may Thou bring peace to Siena,
may Thou be life for Duccio, because he

painted Thou that way». In the hall, in
front of the Maestà is the back side of
the painting divided into 26 panels representing as much episodes of Christ's Passion, ordered from left to right and from
bottom to top: Entrance in Jerusalem;
Washing of the Feet and Last Supper,
Judas's Pact and Christ's leave; the

Prayer in the Garden and the Arrest; Christ before Anna and Peter's denying; Christ beaten and Christ before Caiaphas; Christ accused by the Pharisees and Christ before Pilate; above, Christ sent back to Pilate and Christ before Herod; the Flagellation and the Crowning with thorns; Ascent to Calvary and Pilate's hand washing; Crucifixion; Descent from the Cross and Deposition in the Sepulchre; the Marias at the Sepulchre and Descent in the Limbo; the Apparition in Emmaus and «Noli me tangere».

*Museum of the Opera del Duomo:
1. Mary's funeral; 2. 3. The grandiose altar-piece of the Maestà,
front and back side; 4. Entrance
to Jerusalem (detail of the Maestà's back side), works by Duccio
di Boninsegna.
On pages 80 and 81: Madonna
with Child, by Duccio di Buonin-
segna and Mary's nativity, by Pietro Lorenzetti (detail).*

4

co d'Antonio (1466) and a *Reliquary of St. Clement* (17th cent.). In the glass-cases near the walls, on the right is a wooden *Crucifix* by Giovanni Pisano (ca. 1280), three wooden busts of *Siena's Patron Saints* by Francesco di Valdambrino (1409) and a number of goldsmith's work from the 14th to 17th cent.: by the end wall is the treasure of the Votive chapel, with silver pieces, enamels and rock cristals (17th cent.) and a *Gold rose*, donated by Alexander VII to the Duomo (1658), 5 medieval crosiers, three of which are in ivory, and, on the left, goldsmith's pieces from the 14th to 19th cent. and an *antependium* of decorated silk from the 16th cent.

On top of the stairs, on the opposite side, is the HALL OF THE MADONNA OF MONTAPERTI (wrongly called «big-eyed Madonna»), having in its middle an embossed wood distemper (ca. 1220-30)

with the Madonna in front of whom the «Voting Act» of the town was said on the eve of the battle of Montaperti (4 Sept. 1260). On the walls are a *Madonna of Humility* by Paolo di Giovanni Fei (ca. 1385), four *Saints* from a polyptych by Ambrogio Lorenzetti, nine small panel paintings with *Articles of the Creed*, attributed to Taddeo di Bartolo (ca. 1410), *St. Gerome* by Giovanni di Paolo, four coffin covers by Sodoma, a *polyptych* by Gregorio di Cecco di Luca (1423), a *Madonna with Child* attributed to Sassetta and big wooden doors painted outside with half figures of *Angels* and inside with *Stories of the Cross* previously belonging to an «arliquiera», cabinet for relics, by Benedetto di Bindo (1412). Our visit continues then into the *Alfieri small hall*, so called after Vittorio Alfieri who read there some of his tragedies in 1712. From left to right are a *polyptych* (1479) and an *altar-piece* (1460) by Matteo di Giovanni, *St. Paul* by Beccafumi (1516), a small *altar-piece* by Cristofano Roncalli called «Pomarancio» (1576), a *Crucifixion* and *Christ before Pilate* by Luca Giordano (17th cent.), *Institution of the Eucharist* by G.B. Ramacciotti (17th cent.), *St. Cosma and Damiano* by Raffaello Vanni and the *Transfiguration*, an organ curtain by Girolamo Genga (1510). In the NEXT ROOM, covered by a sumptuous 17th-cent. wall ornament, glass-cases contain a rich series of sacred embroidered vestments (pluvials, chasubles, small habits, etc.) from the 16th to 19th cent. At the end wall, through a small door, we go up a narrow spiral staircase to the loggia and to the top of the «facciatone», from which a beautiful view is offered, both on the Duomo and on the Campo, the whole town and the surrounding countryside can also be seen.

On the piazza del Duomo and at the Cathedral's left side is the ARCHIEPISCOPAL PALACE, rebuilt in Gothic forms in 1727, and, in front of the façade, the CHURCH AND THE HOSPITAL OF S. MARIA DELLA SCALA.

The Spedale, or Hospital, called «della Scala» because it stands before the staircase of the Duomo, is one of the oldest institutions of its kind, founded probably in the 9th century, and certain information about it is reported since the 11th century: during the 14th cent. and the early Renaissance it became one of the major, if not the chief economic power in Siena. Its façade, of stone and fired bricks, dates back to the end of the 13th cent., with one-light mullioned windows

Museum of the Opera del Duomo: 1. Reliquary bust of the 17. cent.; 2. Madonna of the «Voting Act» of Montaperti, by an unknown Sienese painter of the first half of the 13. cent.; 3. Archiepiscopal Palace; 4. Hospital of Santa Maria della Scala.

which replaced two-light ones during the 15th cent. Through the inside vestibule, where, among other things, is the first known painting by Beccafumi representing *Anne meeting Joachim*, we pass into the wide «Pellegrinaio», whose walls are covered by a series of frescoes representing hospital scenes. The value of their authors and the originality of the episodes, crowded with figures wearing beautiful 15th-century costumes and framed by rich architectural sceneries, make them faithful and suggestive documents of the life of those times. From the left wall to the window are: 1 - *Dream of the mother of blessed Sorore* (the mythical founder of the Spedale) *who sees the Staircase of Heaven which is being climbed by orfans received by the Madonna* by Lorenzo di Pietro, called «Vecchietta» (1441); 2 - *Enlargement of the Spedale* by Domenico di Bartolo (1442-43); 3 - *blessed Agostino Novello gives the Rector of the Spedale his robe* by Priamo della Quercia, brother of the great Jacopo (1442); 4 - *Celestinus III grants self-administration rights to the Spedale* by Domenico di Bartolo (1442); 5 and 6 - Two scenes relating to the *Payment in kind and in money to wet-nurses* by Pietro Crogi and Giovanni Navesi (1577); 7 - *Care of the sick*; 8 - *the Distribution of alms*; 9 - *Reception and marriage of orfans*, all by Domenico di Bartolo (1441-43). Another room, which was the old sacristy of the church, contains frescoes by Vecchietta (1449): on the vault is *the blessing Redeemer, the Evangelists, the Doctors of the Church and the Prophets* and, on the walls, *Articles of the Creed*, amid crowded and rich scenes. At the end of the room is a 15th-century tabernacle and a *Virgin of Mercy*, a fresco by Domenico di Bartolo (1444), whose sinopite is displayed on a nearby wall. Other frescoes from the late 14th and 15th cent. are exhibited in different rooms of the Spedale, which will soon be turned into a big cultural centre, mainly a museum, after the remaining wards are moved to a new Polyclinic in «le Scotte» (the Archaeological Museum is presently being moved into the building and its entrance will be on the corner of the square that is already used for temporary exhibits). Through a door almost in the middle of the façade we enter the CHURCH OF THE ANNUNZIATA, with a wide 14th-century interior having a painted lacunar ceiling: over the altar is *Christ resurrected*, a beautiful bronze statue by Vecchietta (1476) and, in the apse, the *Jerusalem bathing-pool* (where sick people were healed), a fresco with great perspective effect by Sebastiano Conca (1732). Above, on the walls, two richly decorated *choirs*, the one to

3

4

the right containing an organ whose sound components are by Giovanni Piffero (among the oldest in Italy and still perfectly functioning, 1517) and with a splendid «front» carved by Giovanni di Pietro called «Castelnuovo» and painted by Bartolomeo di David (1519). Through the following door we go down to the *Oratory of St. Catherine della Notte*, under the vaults of the Spedale, with a small cell where the Saint woman used to rest after assisting sick people: she is portrayed as a sleeping figure in a terra-cotta work attributed to Vecchietta. The Compagnia dei Disciplinati, the oldest in Tuscany (now Società di Esecutori di Pie Disposizioni) has its seat in some adjoining premises, which contain frescoes by Martino di Bartolomeo, Andrea Vanni and others, a beautiful,

wooden *Crucifix*, carved in the late 14th cent., before which, after mystical and spiritual conversations, St. Bernardino received his monastic vocation, a small marble *Madonna* from the 14th cent. and a *triptych* by Taddeo di Bartolo (1400).

Going down the right side of the Spedale, along vicolo S. Girolamo, we reach the CHURCH OF S. SEBASTIANO IN VALLEPIATTA, of the Selva quarter, a graceful construction built on a Greek-cross plan and having a small cylindric dome by Domenico Ponsi, probably from a drawing by Baldassarre Peruzzi (1507), with frescoes by G.P. Pisani, Pierre Sorri and Raffaello Vanni (1627), panel paintings by Benvenuto di Giovanni and Guidoccio Cozzarelli and canvases by Astolfo Petrazzi and Rutilio Manetti.

Leaving Piazza del Duomo and going down via del Capitano and via S. Pietro, we reach BUONSIGNORI PALACE (formerly Bichi and later Tegliacci) built between 1440 and 1458 still in Gothic forms, with an embattled façade of stone and fired bricks, where two orders of very elegant three-light mullioned windows open up. Inside the palace, and in the adjoining palazzetto Brigidi, is the seat of the **PINACOTECA NAZIONALE**, set up there in 1932. It started as a collection in the late 18th cent., and was later enlarged until it represented an almost complete documentation of Sienese painting from the late 12th to the 18th century. In its courtyard, restructured during the 16th cent., are a Roman sarcophagus and an Etruscan urn. The visit, which follows a basic time chronology, begins on the second floor, airier and brighter (only the main works are mentioned here): ROOM

Art gallery - South and south-east areas

National Art Gallery • Church of S. Agostino • Basilica of S. M. dei Servi • Pope Loggias • University Palace • State Archives

1 - w/o no. - *Painted cross*, late 12th cent.; 1 - Altar frontal with *Redeemer and stories of the Cross* dated 1215; 597 - *Painted cross*, early 13th cent.; 8 - Altar frontal of canvas representing the *Transfiguration*, the *Entrance to Jerusalem* and *Lazarus' resurrection*, attributed to Guido da Siena (13th cent.).

ROOM 2: 313 - *St. Francis and 8 episodes from his life* by a follower of Guido; 16 - *Madonna with Child* by Guido da Siena (formerly dated 1262); 7 - Altar frontal by Guido da Siena (with fragment of date: 127.); 14 - *St. John the Baptist on the throne and 12 stories* by unknown Sienese or Umbrian author, with strong Byzantine influences (ca. 1270-80); 15 - *St. Peter on the throne and 6 stories*, a work of very high quality also attributed to the late period of Guido; 4: Diptych with *episodes from the life of St. Francis, St. Clare, St. Catherine of Alexandria and St. Bartholomew* of the school of Guido (ca. 1280); 5 - Diptych with doors with *stories of Blessed Andrea Gallerani, St. Francis and St. Dominic* of the school of Guido; 9 to 13 - Panels representing the *Slaughter of the Innocents and stories of the Passion* by a collaborator of Guido, probably belonging to the wing doors of the «Maestà», formerly in S. Domenico's.

ROOM 3 - In the middle: 35 - Triptych with doors by Duccio di Boninsegna and his collaborators; 47 - Polyptych with *Virgin with Child, 4 Saints and Prophets* by Duccio di Boninsegna and his collaborators, a late work, painted after the «Maestà» (ca. 1315); 28 - Polyptych with the *Madonna and 4 Saints* by Duccio and his collaborators; 39 - *Virgin with Child and 4 Saints* by Ugolino di Nerio; 593 - *Madonna with Child* by the «Maestro of Badia a Isola» (a follower of Duccio); 21 - *Painted cross* by the «Maestro of S. Polo in Rosso» (also attributed to Segna di Bonaventura); 46 - *Painted cross* signed and dated 1345 by Niccolò di Segna.

ROOM 4 - 20 - *Madonna of the Franciscans* by Duccio di Boninsegna, one of the most precious pieces of the whole Gallery, datable back to 1298, probably after the artist spent some time in Paris; its panelled background shows influences of the French miniature painting and the musically unbroken outline, typically Gothic, is combined with still Byzantine figurative patterns; 40 - *Four Saints*, wings of a polyptych by Segna di Bonaventura (signed on St. Paul's sword); 33 - Polyptych of the «Maestro of Città di Castello» (follower of Duccio); 18 - *Madonna on throne with Child*

1

2

by the same author; 592 - *Madonna with Child* by the same author; 36 - *Painted cross* by Ugolino di Nerio; 34 - *Crucifixion with St. Francis* by the same author.

ROOMS 5 AND 6 (now being rearranged). The following works are going to be exhibited there: 593 - *Madonna with Child*, a late work by Duccio (recently attributed to Simone Martini); w/o no. - *Madonna of Mercy* from Vertine, attributed to Niccolò di Segna (recently ascribed to Simone Martini, collaborating with his father-in-law Memmo di Filippuccio); w/o no. - *Madonna with Child* from Lucignano, the most gentle of the Madonnas painted by Simone Martini (ca. 1321), discovered under a rough painting for which the gold and blue of the mantle were removed; w/o no. - *Blessed Agostino Novello and four of his miracles*, from S. Agostino's, one of the masterpieces of Simone Martini (ca. 1330); 595 - *Madonna with Child* by Lippo Memmi; 108 - *Mystical wedding of St. Catherine of Alexandria* by the «Maestro di Palazzo Venezia» (a follower of Simone Martini); w/o no. - *Madonna with Child, St. Peter, St. Paul and an Angel*, fragment of a fresco which was previously in the cloister of S. Domenico and bore once the signature of Lippo Memmi and the date 1350; 115 - Polyptych with half figures by Naddo Ceccarelli (the most important work of this mild and dreaming follower of Simone Martini); 121 - *Madonna with Child and Saints*, small altar-piece by Niccolò di Bonaccorso (ca. 1370); 51 - polyptych with whole figures by Niccolò di ser Sozzo di Stefano and Luca di Tommè, signed and dated 1367; 586 - Polyptych by Luca di Tommè; 103 - Predella made of five parts by Bartolo di Fredi.

ROOM 7 - w/o no. - *St. Peter on the throne between St. Paul and St. John Evangelist* from Sestano, by «Ugolino Lorenzetti» (given name of a painter influenced by Ugolino di Nerio and Pietro Lorenzetti, considered by many to be the same person as the «Maestro d'Ovile»); 61 - *Assumption of the Virgin* by the «Maestro d'Ovile» (probably Bartolomeo Bulgarini, active between 1360 and 1370); 84 - *Dream of Sebach, father of the prophet Elijah - Carmelite hermits at Elijah's well* - w/o no. - *St. Albert gives St. Brocardo the Carmelite Rule* - 83 - *Onorius III approves the Carmelite Rule - Onorius IV grants white cassocks to the Carmelites* - w/o no. - *Madonna with Child between St. Nicola of Bari and the Prophet Elijah* - 578 - *St. Agnese* - 579 - *St. Catherine of Alexandria* - 62 - *St. Taddeus and St. Bartholomew* - 64 - *St. Thomas and St. Jacob*. All these panels belonged to a great altar-piece (two wings and two cusps are now missing), painted in 1328-29 for the church of the Carmine in Siena by Pietro Lorenzetti. This work, still retaining the date and the signature of the artist, is considered his masterpiece for the radiant solemnity of its main part (recently transferred from wood onto canvas) and for his spatial insight of perspective in the wonderful stories of the predella; 79 - 81 - 82 - *St. Bartholomew, St. Cecilia, St. John the Baptist*, panels of a polyptych by Pietro Lorenzetti (the first being dated 1333); 88 - *Annunciation* by Ambrogio Lorenzetti (signed and dated 1344), surprising for its perspective scheme; 70 - 71 - *Seaside town - Castle by a lake* by Ambrogio Lorenzetti (the attribution to Sassetta being unconvincing: these are the only examples of «pure landscape» painting from the 14th cent.); 65 - *Madonna with Child between two Saint women and Doctors of the Church*, a

small but highly remarkable «Maestà» by Ambrogio Lorenzetti (ca. 1340); 605 - *Madonna with Child* called «delle Serre di Rapolano», by Ambrogio Lorenzetti ; 77 - 77a - *Madonna with Child between St. Mary Magdalene and St. Dorothea*, triptych by Ambrogio Lorenzetti (ca. 1330); 116 - *Virgin's Nativity and four Saints* by Paolo di Giovanni Fei, a pleasant work inspired by that of Pietro Lorenzetti in the Museum of Opera del Duomo; 300 - Polyptych signed by Paolo di Giovanni Fei; 145 - *Mystical wedding of St. Catherine of Alexandria and Saints* by Jacopo di Mino del Pellicciaio (signed and dated 1362).

Room 8 - *Adoration of the Magi* a masterpiece by Bartolo di Fredi (ca. 1370-75); 97 to 102 - *Episodes from the life of the Virgin and Saints*, doors, predella and pillars of a polyptych by Bartolo di Fredi (1388) whose central panel is in the Museum of Montalcino; 114 - *Crucifixion between two Prophets*, a triptych by Andrea Vanni (end of the 14th cent.).

Room 9 (Loggia): 67 - *St. Michael Archangel between St. Anthony Abbot and St. John the Baptist*, a triptych attributed to Angiolo Puccinelli from Lucca (ca. 1360); 60 - Small altar by the Florentine Bernardo Daddi (1336); 157 - *Madonna of Humility* by Lorenzo Monaco.

Room 10 (Chapel): *Magdalene*, a maimed terra-cotta statue attributed to Giacomo Cozzarelli (late 15th cent.).

Room 11: 35 - Big *Crucifix* by Taddeo di Bartolo (ca. 1420); 131 - *Annunciation between the St. Cosma and Damiano*, one of the best works by Taddeo di Bartolo (signed and dated 1409); 128 - Small triptych with doors by the same author; 127 - *Adoration of the Magi* by the same author; 132 - *Adoration of the shepherds* by the same author; 219 - *Madonna with Child between the St. Philip and Jacob*, a triptych by Andrea di Bartolo; 140 - *Madonna with Child and the SS. Andrea and Onofrio*, a triptych attributed to Benedetto di Bindo.

Room 12: 200 - *Crucifixion* by Giovanni di Paolo (signed and dated 1440); 198 - Six-panel predella with *stories of the Virgin, St. Peter, Magdalene, St. Galgano and St. Bernard* by Giovanni di Paolo: the predella, remarkable for the cold tones of its colours, belonged, with Saints 199 - 201, to a polyptych for S. Galgano Abbey (ca. 1470); 173 - *St. Nicola of Bari on his throne and Saints*, a polyptych by the same author (signed and dated 1453).

Room 13 - *Madonna of Humility* by

Giovanni di Paolo, one of the artist's most charming creations (ca. 1445); 172 - *The Last Judgement with Heaven and Hell*, a big predella by the same author (ca. 1460-65); 211 - *Presentation to the Temple*, central part of a big altar-piece, now dismembered, commissioned in 1447 by the Pizzicaioli Guild to Giovanni di Paolo for the church of the Spedale; 174 - 174 - 176 - *Presentation to the Temple, Crucifixion and Flight into Egypt*, predella panels by the same author; 212 - *Patient Christ and Triumphant Christ*, an early work (ca. 1426) by the same author; 324 and from 186 to 189 - Polyptych of the *Assumption* from Staggia, the last work by the same author (1475); 95 - *Prophet Elisha* - 87 - *Prophet Elijah*

- 168 - *The Four Patron Saints of Siena* - 169 - *The Four Doctors of the Church* - 166 - *St. Anthony beaten by devils* - 167 - *Last Supper*: all these paintings belonged once to a dismembered altar piece painted between 1423 and 1426 by Stefano di Giovanni called «Sassetta» for the Wool Guild, and represent the first important work of the most important Sienese painter from the 15th century; 203 - *St. Bernardino* by Pietro di Giovanni d'Ambrogio, the most beautiful portrait of the Saint, probably painted in the year of his death (1444).

Room 14: 283 - *Madonna with Child*, a late masterpiece by Matteo di Giovanni (ca. 1490); 280 - *Madonna with Child, St. John Evangelist, St. Jacob and two*

1

2

Angels by the same author (ca. 1480); 286 - *Madonna with Child and four Angels* by the same author (signed and dated 1470); 437 - *Nativity with St. Bernard and St. Thomas of Aquinas* (the names of St. Bernardino and Blessed Ambrogio were added later) by Francesco di Giorgio Martini (signed and painted in 1475); 277 - *Annunciation* by the same author; 288 - *Madonna with Child and an Angel* by the same author; 282 - *Madonna with Child, St. Michael Archangel and St. Bernardino*, a triptych by Neroccio di Bartolomeo (signed and dated 1476); 281 - *Madonna with Child between St. Jerome and St. Bernardino* by the same author, one of the most gentle representations of the Virgin in the whole Sienese painting (ca. 1475); 294 - *Madonna with Child between St. John the Baptist and St. Andrea* by the same author

Art gallery: 1. A seaside town, by Ambrogio Lorenzetti; 2. Blessed Agostino Novello and four of his miracles, by Simone Martini; 3. Blessed Agostino Novello, detail.

(ca. 1495); 278 - *Madonna with Child and four Saints* by the same author (signed and dated 1492).

ROOM 15: 414b - *Adoration of Infant Jesus*, lunette by Matteo di Giovanni; 365 - *Adoration of Infant Jesus*, distemper on canvas by Andrea di Niccolò; 342 - *Adoration of Infant Jesus* by Girolamo di Benvenuto; 279 - *Adoration of the shepherds with St. Galgano and St. Martino* by Pietro di Domenico (signed, ca. 1510); 390 - *Adoration of the shepherds* by the same author; 368 - *Crucifixion* by Andrea di Niccolò (1502).

ROOM 16: 216 - *Crucifixion between St. Ambrose humiliating Theodosius and St. Jerome in the desert*, a predella of a triptych dated 1436 in the Basilica dell'Osservanza after which the «Maestro dell'Osservanza» is named, a contemporary of Sassetta; 265 - *St. Jerome* by Sano di Pietro; 227 - *Assumption of the Virgin*, an early work (before 1444) by Sano di Pietro; 227 - *Madonna adored by Blessed Giovanni Colombini, Angels and Saints*: this is the «polyptych of the Gesuati», signed and dated 1444, the first certain work by Sano di Pietro and his brightest masterpiece (the predella is in the Louvre).

ROOM 17 - It contains only works by Sano di Pietro (apart from a small banner in the middle by Carlo di Giovanni). Among the most significant works are: 241 - *The Virgin commends Siena to Pope Calisto III*, signed and dated 1456 (with two beautiful inscriptions in verses referring to that mystical conversation); 255 - *The Virgin with Child and four Saints*, triptych from Scrofiano signed and dated 1449 (the stories on the predella are particularly worth seeing); 237 - *The Virgin with Child and four Saints* (ca. 1470); 224 - *Madonna with Child and eight Angels* (ca. 1450); 259-260 - *Assumption of the Virgin*, polyptych from S. Petronilla, signed and dated 1479, a late work, remarkable above all for the narrative taste of the seven stories depicted on the predella.

LOGGIA: 164 - *Madonna with Child and five playing Angels*, signed and dated 1433 by Domenico di Bartolo, a masterpiece of basic importance for its features anticipating the Renaissance (an interesting particular is the written passionate appeal of the painter); 171 - *Mystical wedding of St. Catherine of Alexandria, the Baptist and St. Anthony Abbot*, a rare work signed by the Lombard Michelino di Besozzo, one of the most genuine representatives of the «International Gothic».

ROOM 19 - In the middle: 204 - «Arliquiera» or case for relics, painted in 1445 for the Spedale on both door sides (*Saints* outside and *Stories of the Passion* inside)

3

1

by Lorenzo di Pietro called «Vecchietta»; 210 - *Madonna with Child and four Saints*, altar piece painted by the same author for a chapel in the church of St. Maria della Scala which was to house his tomb (1479); 440 - *Crowning of the Virgin*, grandiose altar piece painted in 1472 by Francesco di Giorgio Martini; 428 -

Christ being divested before the Crucifixion painted by the same author and a collaborator, a theme belonging to Northern tradition and very unusual in Italy; 434 - *Ascension of Christ*, a monumental altar piece by Benvenuto di Giovanni signed and dated 1491; *Madonna of Snow and Saints*, signed and dated 1508

Art gallery: 1. Nativity of the Virgin, triptych by Paolo di Giovanni Fei; on the wings, the Saints Jacopo and Catherine d'Alessandria, Bartolomeo and Elisabetta d'Ungheria; 2. Small Maestà, by Ambrogio Lorenzetti.

2

Art gallery: 1. Madonna with Child and Saints Girolamo and Bernardino, by Neroccio di Bartolomeo; 2. Holy Family with Giovannino, by Pinturicchio.

by Benvenuto's son, Girolamo di Benvenuto.

We now go down to the first floor: ROOM 20: *Annunciation*, a rare panel painting by the great miniaturist Girolamo da Cremona; 298 - *Madonna with Child and Saints* by Andrea di Niccolò.

ROOM 23: 426 - *Visitation* by Piero degli Orioli (formerly attributed to Pacchiarotti); 424 - *Madonna with Child and Saints* and 421 - Seven-panel predella by

the same author; 422 - *Christ's Ascension* by the same author; 495 - *Holy Family with St. Giovannino*, a tondo which is considered one of the most beautiful works by Pinturicchio; 43L - *Madonna with Child and Saints*, altar piece signed and dated 1512 by Bernardino Fungai; 333 - 334 - *Release of prisoners - Escape of Aeneas from Troy*, frescoes by Girolamo Genga from Urbino (1509) detached from Palazzo del Magnifico.

ROOM 24: 627 - *Martyrdom of St. Martina*, canvas by Pietro da Cortona.

ROOM 25: (now being rearranged) - 625 - *Martyrdom of St. Ansano*, canvas

signed and dated 1613 by Rutilio Manetti; 626 - *St. Eligio and plague victims* signed and dated 1631 by the same author, one of the best works of this significant Sienese interpreter of Caravaggio's themes.

ROOM 26 (Loggia, being rearranged) - Sculptures of Sienese school from the 14th cent. among which are an altar step with *Stories of Blessed Gioacchino Piccolomini* attributed to Gano di Fazio and reliefs coming from a funeral monument probably by the same author.

ROOMS 27-28-29-30 (now being rearranged) - *Resurrection* by Giorgio Vasari

1

3

2

4

(1550) - 454 - *Portrait of Elisabeth I of England* attributed to Federico Zuccari (also attr. to Cornelius van Ketel); 650 - 651 - 652 - *Charity - Hope - Fortitude* by Andrea Piccinelli called «Bresciani-

Art gallery: 1. Front of the «Arliquiera», by Vecchietta, case for relics, previously in the sacristy of the church of the Spedale; 2. Annunciation, by Francesco di Giorgio Martini; 3. 4. Details of the two wings of the «Arliquiera» with the Capture of Christ and the Ascent to Calvary; 5. Descent from the Cross, by Giovanni Antonio Bassi, called Sodoma.

no»; 444 - *Crowning of the Virgin* by Bartolomeo Neroni called «Riccio»; 403 - *Heaven* by the same author; 410 - *Annunciation and Visitation* by Girolamo del Pacchia (1418); 512 - *Adoration of the Child*, tondo by G. Antonio Bazzi called «Sodoma», one of his best early works (ca. 1503-05); 384 - *Trinity and four Saints* by Domenico Beccafumi (1513).

ROOM 31: 352 - *Christ by the column*, fragment of a fresco scene from the cloister of S. Francesco, one of the most praised creations of Sodoma, showing influences of Leonardo (ca. 1511-14); 420 and 417 - 418 and 419 - *St. Catherine receiving stigmata* and, on the predella, three *stories of the saint woman*, one of the earliest masterpieces by Beccafumi (ca. 1525); 405 - *Virgin's nativity* by the same author, famous for its magical light effects (ca. 1543).

ROOM 32: 413 - *Deposition from the Cross*, one of the earliest masterpieces of Sodoma (1502).

ROOM 37: 401 - 402 - *Christ in the Limbo - Prayer in the garden*, frescoes by Sodoma peeled off in 1842 from the former oratory of S. Croce (ca. 1525); 427 - *Christ's descent to Limbo* by Beccafumi (ca. 1530-35); 423 - *St. Michael Archangel and the Fall of rebel Angels* by the same author (ca. 1528). In the middle: *Annunciating Angel* and *Virgin during the Annunciation*, wood statues gilded in the 17th century attributed to Jacopo della Quercia and his collaborator.

The third floor is also worth visiting, where the Spannocchi collection can be seen, rich in German, Flemish and Italian paintings from the 16th and 17th cent., among which are: 511 - *St. Jerome*, panel painting signed and dated 1514 by Albrecht Dürer; 517 - *Baptist's beheading* by the workshop of Altdorfer (attrib. to the «Maestro of the Historia Federici et Maximiliani»); 534 - *the Tower of Babel* by an unknown Flemish author from the 17th cent.; 643 - *Nativity* by Lorenzo Lotto; 515 - *Susanna at the bath* by Giuseppe Cesari called «Cavalier d'Arpino»; 500 - *Sacred Conversation* by Paris Bordone; 544 - *Annunciation* by the same author (signed); 484 - *Portrait of a young man* by G.B. Moroni; 521 - *St. Francis praying* by Bernardo Strozzi; 552 - *Repenting Magdalene* by Francesco Furini.

On the small square beside the Art Gallery is the CHURCH OF S. PIETRO ALLE SCALE with a beautiful *Flight into Egypt* by Rutilio Manetti (1621) near the high altar, and, on the left wall, is a dismembered polyptych by Ambrogio Lorenzetti.

Through the nearby via Tito Sarroc-

chi we come to PIANO DEI MANTELLINI where, in front of POLLINI PALACE (formerly Celsi), a peculiar building after a plan by Baldassarre Peruzzi, is the 14th-century church of S. NICCOLÒ AL CARMINE, which we enter through a lateral door: inside the church, at the first altar to the right, *Ascension* by Girolamo del Pacchia and, over the opposite altar, *St. Michael Archangel*, a wonderful panel painting by Beccafumi (ca. 1535) and, at the right of the presbytery, «*Madonna dei Mantellini*», a panel painting of Pisan school (ca. 1240) sur-

rounded by four lively *Saints* by Francesco Vanni; on the right wall are remains of 14th-century frescoes and, in the chapel of the Holy Sacrament, on an altar engraved by Marrina, is a *Virgin's Nativity*, late work by Sodoma. Behind the high altar, overlooked by a beautiful 16th-cent. ciborium, is the «*Madonna del Carmine*», a small panel painting of Byzantine school and, in the sacristy, built after a plan attributed to Francesco di Giorgio Martini, *St. Sigismund*, terra-cotta statue by Giacomo Cozzarelli. On the same square is the ORATORY OF

SS. NICCOLO' AND LUCIA, whose interior is decorated with 17th-cent. stucco-works and frescoes and contains a terra-cotta statue of *St. Lucia* by Giacomo Cozzarelli. At the other end of the square, to the right, is the ARCO DELLE DUE PORTE — Arch of the two Gates, belonging to the oldest town walls, through which we go up to via Stalloreggi: there, at the corner with the medieval Bambagini Palace, is a frescoed *Pietà* by Sodoma, called «Madonna of the Crow» because, according to tradition, a plague-spreading crow died here during the 1348 plague. From one side of Pollini Palace we pass into the CHAPEL OF THE S. ANSANO PRISON (containing votive frescoes of the school of Vecchietta), under a gloomy stone tower, allegedly the prison of St. Ansano, then into the CHURCH OF SS. QUIRICO AND GIULITTA, rebuilt in 1596, in whose interior are remains of Roman buildings because this area corresponds to the earliest town settlement: at the left altar is a graceful *Flight into Egypt* by Francesco Vanni. (From the Piano dei Mantellini via S. Marco can be reached, where, on the left, is the CHURCH OF SS. PIETRO AND PAOLO belonging to the Chiocciola town district: in the church is a bright *Crowning of the Virgin* by Brescianino. The street leads down to **Porta S. Marco**, beyond which is piazzale Biringucci with its beautiful lookout on the surrounding countryside). Leaving Piano dei Mantellini through via delle Cerchia, we reach the Gothic CHURCH OF S. AGOSTINO, with a portico by Agostino Fantastici (1819), whose wide and luminous interior was rebuilt in a beautiful Baroque style from 1747 to 1755 from a plan by Luigi Vanvitelli. On the right wall are two altars, the former with the *Communion of St. Jerome* by Astolfo Petrazzi (1631) and the latter with a *Crucifixion* by Perugino (1502-04), a work of basic importance for the subsequent development of painting in Siena. Further along is the Chapel of the Holy Sacrament (in the passage is a statue of *Pius II* by Giovanni Duprè, 1838) which contains a frescoed lunette with a *Madonna with Child and Saints* by Ambrogio Lorenzetti: on the opposite altar, *Epiphany*, among Sodoma's masterpieces (ca. 1530) and, on a wall, *Slaughter of the Innocents*, a dramatic panel painting by Matteo di Giovanni (1482). Back to the nave we see a *Falling of Jesus under the Cross* by Ventura Salimbeni (1612). In the transept, the second chapel, at the right of the high altar, has a majolica floor by the Mazzaburroni family (1488) and important monochrome frescoes have been recently discovered on its walls: they represent the *Nativity of Jesus* and the *Nativity of*

Mary and are by Francesco di Giorgio Martini (1487 to 1496). The overlying lunettes with the *Erythrean and Tiburtine Sybil* are by Luca Signorelli (ca. 1500). In the first chapel to the left is a *seated Madonna with Child*, a beautiful, polychrome and gilded wood group now attributed to Giovanni di Turino (1420) and, on the walls, are two canvases devoted to the Virgin in a «puristic» style, by Giovanni Bruni (1853). The high altar is by Flaminio del Turco with sculptures by Fulvio Signorini (1609) and a ciborium by the Mazzuoli family (1679). In the left chapel are *St. Giuseppe Calasanzio healing a blind child* by Giovanni Bruni (1834) and *Apparition of the Virgin to St. Giuseppe Calasanzio* by Sebastiano Conca (1763). In the second chapel: altar engraved by Marrina with *Christ's Baptism* by Stefano Volpi (1626); to the right, *Temptation of St. Anthony Abbot* by Rutilio Manetti (1630) and, on the left, a frescoed *cenotaph* by Riccio. Over the altar at the transept head is a *St. Nicola of Tolentino*, a wooden statue by Giacomo Cozzarelli (ca. 1480). Again into the nave and advancing towards the entrance, we see the following canvases at the altars:

1. Porta S. Marco; 2. Church of S. Agostino; 3. Church of S. Agostino: «Maestà», fresco by Ambrogio Lorenzetti; 4. Arch of S. Giuseppe; 5. Fountain of the Contrada Onda; 6. Fountain of the Contrada Torre; 7. Piazza del Mercato.

Trinity and Saints by Pietro Sorri (1600), *Baptism of Constantine* by Francesco Vanni (1587), *Mary Immaculate and Saints* by Carlo Maratti (1665-71) and *Adoration of the shepherds* by Giovanni Francesco Romanelli (ca. 1640).

Leaving the garden of S. Agostino and going through via P.A. Mattioli (meanwhile we see on our right the CHURCH OF S. MUSTIOLA, the MUSEUMS OF THE ACADEMIA DEI FISIOCRITICI, containing a rich collection of fossils, mammals, fish species, snakes, birds, mushrooms etc. mostly coming from the Sienese territory and the BOTANICAL GARDEN), we reach the 14th-century **Porta Tufi** attributed to Agnolo di Ventura beyond which, about 300 mt. further, is the CEMETERY OF MISERICORDIA, almost a

museum of Sienese art from the 19th cent., showing sculptures by Duprè and Sarrocchi, as well as paintings by Alessandro Franchi, Cesare Maccari, Pietro Aldi and others.

Again from the garden of S. Agostino we go down from the left to the CHURCH OF S. GIUSEPPE, built in 1522 after a plan of Baldassarre Peruzzi, with a façade by Benedetto Giovannelli (1643): in the adjoining premises of the Onda district is a *gallery of plaster casts* of Giovanni Duprè's works. Then we pass under the Arco di S. Giuseppe, coming, through via Duprè, to the market square onto which the back of Public Palace looks. Leaving the square and going up via Salicotto, where the ORATORY OF S. GIACOMO belonging to the Torre district can

be seen, and passing by the CONVENT AND CHURCH OF S. GIROLAMO (frescoes by Girolamo del Pacchia and *Crowning of the Virgin* by Sano di Pietro), we finally reach the 13th-cent. **Basilica of S. Maria dei Servi**, with its unfinished façade standing beside a Romanesque bell tower. The beautiful interior with a nave and two aisles, divided by columns, was restored in the late 15th or early 16th cent. by Ventura Turapilli, probably after a plan by Peruzzi: the apse and the transept are still in Gothic style from the 14th century. At the second altar of the right aisle is a *Madonna del Bordone* dated 1261 and signed by the Florentine Coppo di Marcovaldo who, according to tradition, painted it in exchange for his release after being captured at the battle of Montaperti (flesh-colours were

repainted in the early 14th cent. by a follower of Duccio). At the third altar is a *Virgin's nativity* by Rutilio (or Domenico) Manetti. At the fourth a *Slaughter of Innocents* by Matteo di Giovanni (1491) and, on a wall, an *Adoration of the shepherds* by Taddeo di Bartolo (1404). In the transept, in the second chapel to the right of the choir, is a *Slaughter of the Innocents*, a dramatic fresco by Pietro Lorenzetti: over the high altar a *Crowning of the Virgin* by Bernardino Fungai (1500) and, on top of the triumphal arch, *Pietà*, a terra-cotta bas-relief by Giacomo Cozzarelli. In the second chapel to the left of the choir are a *Dancing Salome* and an *Assumption of St. John*, frescoes by Pietro Lorenzetti and his collaborators; over the head altar *Madonna del Manto* by Giovanni di

Paolo (1436). On the internal transept walls are the *Annunciating Angel* and *Virgin during the Annunciation*, early canvases by Francesco Vanni. At the second altar of the left aisle, «*Madonna di Belvedere*» by Jacopo di Mino del Pellicciaio (1364) and, over the first, *Annunciation*, a work by Francesco Vanni whose gentleness reminds of Barocci's style. The *Painted Cross* on the rear-façade wall is ascribed to Niccolò di Segna. Behind the apse of the Servi is the ORATORY OF THE HOLY TRINITY, elegantly decorated with 16th-century stuccoworks and the 17th and 18th cent. frescoes by Raffaello Vanni, Ventura Salimbeni and Giuseppe Nasini: in adjoining rooms are a *Madonna* by Sano di Pietro and a beautiful tabernacle by Neroccio di Bartolomeo (ca. 1495). From the small square a short flight of stairs leads down to via Roma, in front of the CHURCH OF THE SANTUCCIO (frescoes by Ventura Salimbeni), next to the seat of the *Società di Esecutori di Pie Disposizioni*: an adjoining Museum contains a *Painted Cross* from the 13th cent. and several panel paintings, among which are a small triptych with *Stories of the Passion* attributed to Duccio, a *Madonna* and two *Saints* by Niccolò di ser Sozzo (first half of the 14th cent.), a lunette with *St. Catherine leading Gregory XI back to Rome* by Girolamo di Benvenuto, a *Madonna* by Sodoma and a rare small altar piece with figures on small slabs of gilded glass attributed to Niccolò di ser Sozzo. At the other side is a palace containing the MUSEO BOLOGNA, a collection recently donated to the Society, exhibiting Etruscan objects, pieces of furniture and variously dated paintings of minor importance. Then we reach **Porta Romana**, an example of beautiful Gothic architecture, with barbican, attributed to Agnolo di Ventura (1327): the frescoes once decorating the gate were destroyed by the war in 1944 and peeled off fragments are preserved in the Basilica of S. Francesco. Outside the gate lies the VALLI suburb with its two churches: the 15th-century S. MARIA DEGLI ANGIOLI (containing an altar piece by Raffaellino del Garbo, 1502), and the Romanesque S. MARIA IN BETLEM, with an interesting façade of fired bricks.

Back to via Roma and walking towards the town centre we see, on a small square to the right, the 17th-century façade of the CHURCH DEL REFUGIO (containing canvases by Francesco Vanni, Ventura Salimbeni and Rutilio Manetti) after which is the S. GALGANO PALACE (1474), with a beautiful façade having two orders of two-light mullioned windows, attributed to Giuliano da Maiano. At the cross-roads is a column

bearing a Sienese She-wolf from 1470 and after a gate called «il Ponte di Romana» the street takes on the name of via Pantaneto; turning right shortly afterwards into via dei Pispini, we get to an open space with a 1534 fountain where the CHURCH OF S. SPIRITO stands (1498), made of fired bricks and with a massive dome built in 1508 after a plan attributed to Giacomo Cozzarelli. In the church interior the first chapel to the right, called «degli Spagnoli», is completely frescoed by Sodoma (1530) who depicted there *St. James riding over the*

Basilica of S. Maria dei Servi: 1. The architectonic group of buildings; 2. The interior; 3. Madonna with Child, by Coppo di Marcovaldo; 4. Slaughter of the Innocents, by Pietro Lorenzetti; 5. Porta Romana.

defeated Saracens above, *Mystical clothing of St. Ildefonso* on the lunette and *St. Sebastian* and *St. Anthony Abbot* on the sides: behind a screen is a *Nativity scene* in coloured terra-cotta by brother Ambrogio della Robbia. 2nd chapel, *St. Vincenzo Ferreri*, wooden statue by Giacomo Cozzarelli. 3rd chapel, *Mary's crowning* by Beccafumi (1540). 4th chapel, over the altar, *St. Giacinto in glory* by Francesco Vanni and, on the walls, *Miracles of St. Giacinto*, one of the most beautiful frescoes by Ventura Salimbeni (1600). On the apse's pilasters are four *Saints* by Rutilio Manetti (1608) and, in the apse, the *Pentecost*, a fresco by Giuseppe Nasini. In the left aisle, 3rd chapel, *Mary's crowning* by Girolamo del Pacchia, *Crucifix* by Sano di Pietro and *Madonna* by Andrea Vanni. 1st chapel, *Our Lady of the Assumption between St. Francis and St. Catherine*, a remarkable panel painting attributed to Matteo Balducci (1509), a painter, however, without a strong personality.

After passing the ORATORY OF S. GAETANO (1670) in the Nicchio district, we go down from piazza S. Spirito to the 14th-cent. **Porta Pispini** (also called «Sanviene» because, according to tradition, the relics of St. Ansano were brought to Siena through it in 1107). Back into via Pantaneto we pass by the CHURCH OF S. GIORGIO with a façade by Pietro Cremoni (1741: inside is an *Ascent to*

Calvary by Francesco Vanni, who was buried here in 1610) and a Romanesque bell tower from 1260 with 38 windows. Slightly further ahead appears the outline of the **Logge del Papa**, an elegant, three-arched Renaissance construction, commissioned to Antonio Federighi (1462) by Pius II in honour of his family, to the right of which is the CHURCH OF S. MARTINO by G.B. Pelori (1537) with a façade by Giovanni Fontana (1613). Inside the church, on the right, a votive panel painting of the *Battle of Camollia* (1526) by Giovanni di Lorenzo Cini; over the second altar is a *Circumcision*, a masterpiece by Guido Reni (1635-40), on the third *Martyrdom of St. Bartholomew* by Guercino inside a marble framework by Marrina; over the opposite altar, *Nativity* by Beccafumi (ca. 1523), at the 1st altar *St. Ivone* by Raffaello Vanni and at the 2nd a *Crucifixion*, a repainted wooden group from the 15th cent. The statues at the altars of the transept are by Giuseppe Mazzuoli.

(Along one side of S. Martino runs via del Porrione, where the ORATORY OF MISERICORDIA stands: the building contains a *St. Anthony Abbot* attributed to Giovanni di Turrina, two beautiful wooden statues representing the *Annunciation* attributed to Marrina and a panel painting by Girolamo del Pacchia).

Still along via Pantaneto, here taking on the name of Banchi di Sotto, we see

1

2

3

4

5

6

State Archives: 1. The oldest cover of the Biccherna collection (1258). The Camerlengo is Abbot Ugo, Monk at S. Galgano; 2. The Virgin recommends Siena to Jesus, a Gabella cover, by Neroccio di Bartolomeo (1480); 3. The Virgin protects Siena during an earthquake, by Francesco di Giorgio Martini (detail of a Biccherna cover, 1467); 4. The Commune finances in peacetime and in wartime, Gabella cover by Benvenuto di Giovanni (1468); 5. St. Michele Archangel fights against the dragon, Gabella cover attributed to «Maestro dell'Osservanza» (1444); 6. The lady with the gold-quilted mantle, a register cover attributed to Taddeo di Bartolo.

on the right, the **University Palace** (formerly a Jesuit convent), in whose courtyard are the tomb of jurist *Guglielmo di Ciliano* by Goro di Gregorio (ca. 1325-30), a monument to gonfalonier *Giulio Bianchi* by Pietro Tenerani (1842) and a monument to the *Soldiers who died at Curtatone and Montanara* (29 May 1848) by Raffello Romanelli (1894). Behind the University Palace is the CHURCH OF S. VIGILIO ALLA SAPIENZA (ceiling frescoed by Raffaello Vanni and canvas with *St. Ignazio* by Mattia Preti) and, in front of it, is the austere PICCOLOMINI PALACE, the most beautiful Renaissance palace in Siena, begun in 1469 by Pietro Paolo del Borrina, probably after a plan by Bernardo Rossellino. In the palace are also the **State Archives**, very rich in documents of historical and artistic importance (among which is Boccaccio's testament), where the **Galleria delle Tavolette dipinte** can be visited, i.e. a collection of wooden covers for registers of the Biccherna and the Gabella, the two main tax offices in the old Sienese state. The displayed covers, forming a collection of small paintings which is unique in the world, were renewed twice a year with coats of arms and historical, allegorical and religious scenes painted by the greatest artists of the times, from 1228 to 1689. Among the miniature treasures of the Archives is the famous *Caleffo dell'Assunta* with the title page «illuminated» by Niccolò di ser Sozzo (1334). Via Banchi di Sotto leads finally to the Croce del Travaglio.

From the Croce del Travaglio we go up along Banchi di Sopra to piazza Tolomei overlooked by 13th-cent. **Tolomei Palace**, the oldest Gothic palace in Siena with a beautiful stone façade having two orders of two-light mullioned windows, in front of which are a column bearing a *Sienese She-wolf* made of tin from 1610 and the Romanesque CHURCH OF S. CRISTOFORO, where the «Consiglio della Campana» used to gather before the Public Palace was built. The church façade was rebuilt in 1779 and it contains two statues of *Blessed Bernardo Tolomei* and *Blessed Nera Tolomei* by Giuseppe Silini. Inside the church, at the right altar, we can see a wood 14th-cent. *Crucifix*, and next to it a *St. George* by the «Maestro dell'Osservanza» and *St.*

From the Croce del Travaglio to S. Francesco and Piazza Salimbeni

Tolomei Palace • Basilica of S. Francesco • Piazza Salimbeni

Christopher by Sano di Pietro. Over the high altar is the *Blessed Tolomei in glory*, a marble group by Bartolomeo Mazzuoli (18th cent.) and, on the walls of the presbytery, *St. Galgano* in terra-cotta, of the school of Federighi and a *Madonna with Child* of stucco by the workshop of Jacopo della Quercia, as well as a 15th-cent. fresco. The altar piece over the left altar, *Madonna with Child and the Saints Luca and Romualdo* is by Girolamo del Pacchia (1508). Going along the left side of the church and turning down via del Moro, we enter, at No. 2, a typical small cloister from the 12th cent. Leaving via del Moro and turning into via Lucherini, we reach piazza Provenzano where the beautiful COLLEGIATE CHURCH OF S. MARIA DI PROVENZANO by Flaminio del Turco stands (1595), after a plan by the Carthusian brother Damiano Schifardini with a stone façade and extrados cupola, specially built to contain a revered Madonna of terra-cotta, the fragment of a 15th-century *Pietà* which was hit by a Spanish arquebus'shot. Inside, on the right, the *Mass of St. Cerbone* by Rutilio Manetti (1630) and, at the right altar of the transept, *Vision of St. Catherine* by Francesco Rustici (1613).

Walking by one side of the church along via Provenzano Salvani we turn left into via del Giglio where the 13th-century CHURCH OF S. PIETRO A OVILE, which contains highly remarkable works of art, stands. Over the left altar is a rare 14th-century copy of the famous *Annunciation* by Simone Martini (1333) attributed to Matteo di Giovanni (ca. 1455); behind the high altar we can see a *Painted cross* by Giovanni di Paolo and, in the left chapel, *Crucifix* with *weeping Madonna and St. John Evangelist*, wood statues by Domenico di Niccolò dei Cori polychromed by Martino di Bartolomeo (1415). Over the left altar is a *Madonna with Child* from the mid 14th cent., after which the «Maestro d'Ovile» was named (temporarily in the Seminary of Montarioso). Near the church we turn right into via dei Rossi which leads, after the Arch of S. Francesco, in front of the **Basilica of S. Francesco**, begun in 1326 and finished in 1479, probably with the collaboration of Francesco di Giorgio Martini. Its façade, originally unfinished, was completely rebuilt in false Gothic style from 1894 to 1913, and the interior was restructured as well (1885-92): during the works, Baroque altars supporting remarkable paintings were

demolished, and now those canvases are going to be placed again into the church. The construction, whose plan is in the shape of an Egyptian cross or a Tau, has a very wide nave and a transept with four chapels at each choir side. *Playing angels* by Sassetta, previously on the underside of a tabernacle arch on Porta Romana (1450), and fragments of a fresco by Sodoma (1531), detached from Porta Prispini, have been recently placed on the rear-façade wall. Then we see sculptures formerly belonging to early 14th-century monuments. The ancient portal of the façade, after a magnificent drawing attributed to Francesco di Giorgio Martini has been walled up in the left wall and, further ahead, there is a *Crucifix with St. Jerome* by Girolamo di Benvenuto, a peeled off fresco coming from the ancient cemetery. On the right wall are some 14th-century frescoes such as a *Visitation* and a 14th-century tomb of the Tolomei family. After entering the sacristy (a peeled off fresco with *Madonna and St. Anne* by Cesare Maccari, 1890) we pass into the chapel of the Sacrament, which belongs to the convent, where a false-polyptych fresco by Lippo Vanni (ca. 1370) can be seen. At the end of the right transept wing is a *St. Francis*, a marble statue attributed to Francesco di Valdambrino formerly on the façade portal. In the 3rd chapel, at the right of the choir, the *Assumption of Magdalene*, a relief pediment reminding of the style of Giovanni d'Agostino, in the 2nd, a beautiful bas-relief tomb of *Cristoforo Felici* by Urbano da Cortona (1462), in the 1st, a *Madonna with Child* by Andrea Vanni and, in the choir, inside shell-like clipei - shields -, busts of *Pius II's parents* attributed to Antonio Federighi: the stained glass-window of the big four-light mullioned window representing the *Approval of the Franciscan rule* was remade in 1952 by the Zettler Workshop of Munich. In the first chapel at the choir's right, there is a *Crucifixion*, a detached fresco by Pietro Lorenzetti, a dramatic masterpiece; in the third, the *Martyrdom of Franciscan friars in Thanah* and *Ludovico da Tolosa leaving Boniface VIII*, peeled off frescoes by Ambrogio Lorenzetti, admirable for their scenic arrangement and the liveliness of figures, dressed with Eastern and contemporary costumes. In the last chapel, *Madonna with Child*, a fresco attributed to Jacopo di Mino del Pellicciaio. In front of it is the chapel of the Sacred Hosts, in

4

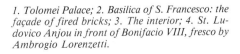

1. Tolomei Palace; 2. Basilica of S. Francesco: the façade of fired bricks; 3. The interior; 4. St. Ludovico Anjou in front of Bonifacio VIII, fresco by Ambrogio Lorenzetti.

which 223 consecrated Hosts are kept, which were miraculously preserved after a theft in 1730: it has a beautiful graffito floor with *Cardinal Virtues* by Marrina. Through a door on the right side of the nave we enter a big 16th-century cloister where, amid other sculpture fragments, the beautiful portal of the Petroni chapel, dated 1336, is walled up, with its lunette having a *Madonna with Child between St. Francis and Blessed Pietro da Siena* attributed to Domenico d'Agostino. The convent had once two more cloisters: a 15th-century one, now belonging to the Faculty of Law, and a 16th-century one, now in the headquarters of the Paramilitary Police. The bell tower of fired bricks is by Paolo Posi (1763).

On the same square rises the ORATORY OF S. BERNARDINO, built on the spot where the Saint used to preach, with a portal from 1574. The lower oratory has a vault frescoed by Francesco Vanni (1580) and a series of lunettes with *Stories* and *Miracles of St. Bernardino* by Sienese painters from the 17th cent.; the most remarkable ones are by Ventura Salimbeni (*The Saint raises from the death a child killed by a bull* and *The Saint raises a drowned child*, 1602). On top of the stairs is a *Madonna with Child* of coloured stucco by the school of Jaco-

po della Quercia and, in the vestibule, besides a banner painted on either side attributed to Arcangelo Salimbeni, is an admirable small bas-relief with a *Madonna with Child between two Angels* signed by Giovanni d'Agostino, a work of basic importance for the understanding of this very refined painter from the 14th century. We continue our visit to the upper oratory: a sort of treasury chest because it represents the most beautiful example of mature Renaissance art in Siena for the elegance of its decorations of gilded wood and stucco on a blue background carried out by Ventura Turapilli (1496) and for the high quality paintings covering its sides.

They are by Girolamo del Pacchia, who in 1518 painted *Mary's nativity, St. Bernardino* and the two panels of the *Annunciation*, by Sodoma, who painted *St. Ludovico, Presentation to the temple, St. Antony, Visitation, Assumption, St. Francis* and a wonderful *Mary's crowning* (1518), and by Beccafumi, author of a *Wedding of Mary* and of a *Virgin's passage* (1519) and a panel painting behind the altar, *Madonna in glory among Saints* (1537). A relic of St. Bernardino's heart is preserved in the oratory, as well as one of the tablets with *Christ's monogram*, which the Saint used to show during his preachings.

Sorri, A. Casolani, S. Folli and R. Manetti) and the «CASA DELLA CONSUMA», where the famous «brigata spendereccia», remembered by Dante, spent 200,000 golden fiorins in 20 months, are to be found.

To the left of the cross-roads with via Vallerozzi, via dell'Abbadia leads to a small square, overlooked by the massive back of the ROCCA DEI SALIMBENI and where the CHURCH OF S. DONATO lies (12th cent.), an old abbey of the Vallombrosian brothers, whose interior is interesting for a high cupola supported by arches and angular squinches: at the high altar, a *tabernacle* and marble *Angels* by Giuseppe Mazzuoli and, in the apse, *Hell*, a fresco by the Neoclassical Luigi Ademollo: in the adjoining 18th-century oratory of Sacri Chiodi, *Madonna with Child* by Andrea Vanni. Our visit continues along via dell'Abbadia and then to the right through via dei Rossi which leads to Banchi di Sopra, the busiest and most elegant street of Siena (with the Gothic BICHI RUSPOLI PALACE and CINUGHI PALACE, and 1577 GORI PANNILINI PALACE). Banchi di Sopra ends at piazza Salimbeni in the middle of which stands a monument to the economist *Sallustio Bandini* by Tito Sarrocchi (1882); on the right is the beautiful SPANNOCCHI PALACE by Giuliano da Majano (1473: the original façade looks onto Banchi di Sopra, while the front looking on the square is an imitation by Giuseppe Partini, 1880); on the left is TANTUCCI PALACE also called della DOGANA del Riccio (1548), and, on the background, the old ROCCA DEI SALIMBENI, with a façade widely restructured by Giuseppe Partini (1872). Inside the stronghold is the Head Office of the **Monte dei Paschi di Siena**, one of the oldest and most important Italian banks, founded in 1472 (this name comes from the pasture lands (pascoli) of the Maremma, once serving as guarantee for financial transactions). The bank owns, apart from major historical archives, a rich collection of art works with precious 14th-cent. paintings by Sassetta, by the «Maestro dell'Osservanza», Giovanni di Paolo, Benvenuto di Giovanni, Fungai, Beccafumi, Pietro degli Orioli, Lorenzo Rustici, Raphael, Francesco Vanni, Manetti, Mei, by the greatest Sienese masters from the 18th to the 20th century, and sculptures from the 14th and 15th cent. by Federighi, Antonio Rossellino, Duprè and others.

1. Oratory of S. Bernardino: Presentation of Mary in the Temple, by Sodoma; 2. Piazza Salimbeni and Salimbeni Palace, seat of the bank Monte dei Paschi di Siena; 3. The house in which St. Catherine (1340-1380) was born and lived; the Saint was canonized in 1461 by Pius II and proclaimed co-patron of Italy in 1939 by Pius XII.

Starting from the Arch of S. Francesco and going down via del Comune, we reach the 14th-century **Porta Ovile** beyond which is the 1262 FONTE - fount - D'OVILE: not far from here, within the town walls, is the 14th-cent. FONTE NUOVA, with pointed arches of fired bricks. Going up the steep via Vallerozzi, to the right we see the CHURCH OF S. ROCCO, in the Lupa district, from the 16th cent., whose interior is richly decorated with

Stories of Job and contains a chapel with *Stories of St. Roch* by Rutilio Manetti and Francesco Rustici: in the seat of the Contrada, *Apparition of the Virgin to St. Roch*, one of the most beautiful canvases by Ventura Salimbeni (signed and dated 1603). Further ahead we come to a cross-roads: to the right is via della Stufa Secca leading to via Garibaldi, where the ORATORY OF S. SEBASTIANO (containing frescoes with *Stories of the Saint* by P.

The Northern quarters

Santuario Cateriniano • Fonte Branda • Basilica of S. Domenico • Fountain of S. Barbara • Porta Camollia

A few metres after the Croce del Travaglio we reach Piazza Indipendenza, on the right, with its LOGGIA DELL'INDIPENDENZA by Archimede Vestri (1887) behind which is the embattled PALAZZO BALLATI loverlooked by a massive stone tower. In front of it is the entrance to the THEATRE OF THE ACCADEMIA DEI ROZZI with an elegant hall built in 1816 by Alessandro Doveri and restored in 1874. We turn right into Via di Diacceto where a suggestive vision of the Basilica of S. Domenico is offered from an overbridge; then we go down Via della Galluzza, to the right, the most picturesque street in medieval Siena, crossed by eight arches, which leads to the PORTICO DEI COMUNI (1941): besides the arcade is the **Santuario Cateriniano**, built on the house where St. Catherine was born (25 March 1347) and where his father Jacopo Benincasa had his dye-workshop. The different rooms of the house, on different floors, were turned into oratories starting from 1465 by the Confraternity of St. Catherine and in the 17th cent. the Church of the Crocifisso was built on the old garden. The construction was specially built to contain the *Crucifix*, a panel painting from the late 12th-cent. Pisan school, in front of which in 1375, according to tradition, the Saint received stigmata in the Pisan church of S. Cristina.

The work was then secretly transported to Siena in 1565. On the vault is *St. Catherine in Glory* by Giuseppe Nicola Nasini (1703) and on the walls are 18th-cent. frescoes representing the Saint. On the left transept altar is the *Saint being received by the Virgin* by Rutilio and Domenico Manetti (1638) and on the right one the *Saint before the Pope in Avignon* by Sebastiano Conca. In a room adjoining the sacristy, we can see the *Stigmatization of the Saint*, a banner by Rutilio Manetti (1630) and four beautiful coffin heads by Francesco Vanni (1591). At the left of the small cloister we enter the «kitchen oratory», an elegant 16th-cent. space with a majolica floor of the 17th cent. by Girolamo di Marco vasaio and an engraved ceiling after a plan by Riccio. Over the altar, which contains the remains of a fireplace onto which St. Catherine as a child fell, coming out miraculously unscathed, is a panel painting with the *Saint's stigmata* by Bernardino Fungai (1496) inside a framing painted by Riccio. On the walls are 17 paintings in this order starting from the altar's right: 1 - *The Saint gives her tunic to begging Jesus* by Riccio (1571); 2 - *St. Bernardino* by Pietro Aldi (1872); 3 - *Mystical wedding of the Saint* by Arcangelo Salimbeni (1579); 4 - *The Papal See being moved to Rome by Gregory XI on the Saint's advice* by Pomarancio (1583); 5 - *The Saint exhorting the Roman people to faithfulness to Urban VI* by Alessandro Casolani (1583); 6 - *Blessed Andrea Gallerani* by the same author; 7 - *Vision of Christ by the column* by Rutilio Manetti; 8 - *The Saint receiving a crown of thorns from Jesus* by Pietro Sorri; 9 - *Saint's canonization*, oil fresco by Francesco Vanni (1600); 10 - *The Holy Spirit appearing over the praying Saint* by Rutilio Manetti; 11 - *Jesus replacing his heart with the Saint's* by Francesco Vanni; 12 - *Blessed Giovanni Colombini* attributed to Casolani; 13 - *The Saint freeing a possessed woman* by Pietro Sorri (1587); 14 - *Communion of the Saint* by Pomarancio (1582); 15 - *The Saint comforting tortured evil-doers* by Lattanzio Bonastri (1589); 16 - *Blessed Ambrogio Sansedoni* by Gaetano

3

Marinelli (1885); 17 - *Jesus gives the Saint a small cross after she gave Him her tunic* by Riccio (1571). If we go downstairs we reach the «chamber oratory», with a panel painting of *Stigmatization* by Girolamo di Benvenuto over its altar and, on the walls, a refined and luminous cycle of frescoes with *Stories of the Saint* by Alessandro Franchi (1896): according to tradition the Saint used to sleep in the adjoining narrow cell, where a statue representing her, by P. Repossi (1940), can be seen, as well as some objects belonging to her and the stone she used as a pillow. After going down another flight of stairs, to the right after a vestibule, we enter the old store of the Benincasa, turned into the church of St. Catherine in the 15th cent. Over the altar is a wooden statue of *St. Catherine* showing deep

devotion, a masterpiece by Neroccio di Bartolomeo (1475). The five angels laying a cloth on the altar were frescoed by Sodoma (1520) and the overlooking lunette with the *Stigmatization* is by Girolamo del Pacchia (1525) who frescoed, on the right wall, the *Saint freeing some Dominicans attacked by bandits* and *St. Agnes of Montepulciano in the bier, lifting a foot which St. Catherine was about to kiss*. On the left wall are frescoes representing the *Healing of Matteo Cenni*, by Vincenzo Tamagni and the *Blinding of the Florentine hired to kill the Saint* by Ventura Salimbeni (1604). The three frescoes on the rearfaçade, presumably representing the Saint, are by Sebastiano Folli (1607). A narrow flight of stairs leads down to a cellar where the miracle of the never-empty barrel took

place and on the other side of the landing is the Museum of the Nobil Contrada dell'Oca, with a rich hall containing interesting pieces pertaining to the Palio. Going out onto Via S. Caterina we admire the Sanctuary with the 15th-cent. façade of the church, widely restructured in the last century (the sculptures on the portal are attributed to Urbano da Cortona) and flanked by the seat of the Contrada, whose 16th-century portal is overlooked by a two-storey loggia. The street leads then down to the **Fonte Branda**, which lies in a picturesque position at the foot of the hill where the red mass of S. Domenico stands. The fountain, built in the 12th cent., has a basin covered by vaults from 1246 and having on the front three pointed arches decorated with stone lions, while the embattled crowning was added during a restoration.

Through Via dei pittori, in front of the Portico dei Comuni, we reach Via delle Terme which, turning left, leads to Via della Sapienza. There, at the beginning of the street, is the church of S. PELLEGRINO ALLA SAPIENZA (having a vault with graceful *Stories of the Virgin*, frescoed in the 18th cent. by Giuliano Traballesi, and with panel paintings representing *St. Peter*, *St. Paul*, from the 14th cent., *Blessed Andrea Gallerani*, a highly refined image by a follower of Simone Martini and a 14th-century ivory tabernacle), and then the MUSEO ARCHEOLOGICO NAZIONALE (National Archaeological Museum), presently being moved to a wing of the Spedale of S. Maria della Scala. The museum, set up in 1956, contains furnishings and works of art of Prehistoric, Etruscan and Roman times from the Bargagli Petrucci, Bonci Casuccini and Chigi Zonzadari collections and from excavations in Siena and other areas at the south of the town (Chiusi, Chianciano, Montepulciano, Sarteano etc.). Of particular interest are a rich series of small Etruscan urns, the clay decorations of a temple in Poggio Civitate (Murlo, 6th cent. B.C.), the «sarcophagus of the Chigi Muses» of Hadrian age, from an original by Praxiteles, the «Pseudo-Seneca», a Roman head of the 1st cent. A.D., craters with black and red figures among which is an amphora with warriors on a biga and Maenads and Satyrs of the 6th cent. B.C.

Then we reach the BIBLIOTECA COMUNALE DEGLI INTRONATI, founded in 1759 and containing ca. 350,000 volumes, among which are 1,000 incunabula, 6,000 manuscripts and miniated codices and a number of drawings and prints. The most interesting pieces are a Byzantine *Evangeliary* of the 10th cent. coming from the imperial palace of Constantinople with an admirable binding of silver-gilt and figured enamels, a Franciscan *Breviary* miniated by Sano di Pietro, an *Antiphonary* miniated by Giovanni di Paolo, a *Roman Pontifical* with French miniatures from the 15th cent., a *Book of Hours* miniated by Littifredi de' Corbizi (1494), two notebooks with drawings by Francesco di Giorgio Martini, a sketch-book with drawings by Giuliano da Sangallo and a rich series of miniated codices of the 11th-15th centuries.

Via della Sapienza ends into Piazza S. Domenico - the former poggio di Camporegio - and is limited by the left side of the **Basilica of S. Domenico** which, with its Gothic austere forms made of bricks, resembles a fortress. Founded in 1225, about ten years after the Saint's stay in Siena, the construction had its main wing finished by 1265 and a transept was added starting from the middle of the following century: the 1340 bell tower was originally much higher and it was shortened after an earthquake in 1798. Since a chapel, the cappella delle Volte, was already there when the basilica was built, with its unfinished façade next to it, the only possible entrance was only through a side door. To the right, immediately after the entrance and up three steps, is the cappella delle Volte, a place where St. Catherine's visions and her mystical conversations with Jesus occurred. Over the altar is a *Portrait of the Saint with a devout*, fresco by Andrea Vanni, considered the only work on this subject based on reliable observation considering that the painter actually knew the Virgin of Fontebranda. On the wall opposite the altar, we can see the *Saint's canonization* by Mattia Preti (1673), with two canvases on its sides, *Gift of a dress to a beggar* and *Jesus offering the Saint a small cross* by Crescenzio Gambarelli (1602), also the author of the big canvases of the *Saint's passing away* and the *Office declamation with Jesus* which, together with *Apparition to St. Rosa of Lima* by Deifebo Burbarini, hang on the long wall. Down into the church we see, at the 1st altar, *Apparition of the Virgin to the Blessed Andrea Gallerani* by Stefano Volpi (1640) followed by a wooden Crucifix of the 14th cent. over a *Pietà*, a 15th-cent. wooden group; at the 2nd, *Mary's nativity*, probably the masterpiece of Alessandro Casolani (1584). Then we come to the chapel of St. Catherine, built in 1460 to preserve the

3

4

Santuario Cateriniano: 1. Entrance with the Portico dei Comuni; 2. Small loggia giving way into the crucifix oratory, attributed to Baldassarre Peruzzi; 3. Crucifix oratory; 4. Fonte Branda, the most famous fountain in Siena. On pages 108-109: panoramic view of the town from S. Domenico, with the Duomo and the Torre del Mangia.

1

2

Beside the fresco is a beautiful panel painting with the *Adoration of shepherds and Angels* by Francesco di Giorgio Martini (ca.1480) overlooked by a lunette with *Christ emerging from the sepulchre between St. Michael and Magdalene* by Matteo di Giovanni and a predella with five stories, among the best works of Bernardino Fungai. We pass into the transept which has three chapels on each side of the choir. Over the altar at one end, between two Baroque, stucco statues of *St. Thomas* and *St. Jacopo di Mevania* is a canvas representing *Blessed Ambrogio Sansedoni interceding with St. Dominic on behalf of the souls in Purgatory* by Francesco Rustici called «Rustichino» (ca.1613). In the 1st chapel are fragments of 14th- century frescoes, the 2nd is the chapel of the German Nation with a marble *Crucifix between St. Barbara and Magdalene* and a number of memorial stones, mostly of German students in the 16th cent., and the 3rd has a panel painting of the *Virgin between Angels and Saints* by Matteo di Giovanni. On the right wall of the airy choir is a big, dramatic canvas of the *Killing of St. Peter Martyr*, the most significant work by Arcangelo Salimbeni (1579) and on the left *St. Thomas before the Pope* by Galgano Perpignani (18th cent.): over the altar is a very elegant ciborium flanked by two *Angels bearing candelabra*, a rare works by the Florentine Benedetto da Majano (ca.1480). In 4th-chapel is a wooden statue of *St. Anthony Abbot* from 1425 attributable to Turino di Sano (or to his son Giovanni). On the walls of the 5th chapel are two admirable panel paintings: *Virgin with Child, four Saints and two Angels* and a lunette with *Dead Christ supported by Angels* by Benvenuto di Giovanni, and *St. Barbara on the throne between St. Catherine of Alexandria and Magdalene*, a radiant masterpiece by Matteo di Giovanni (1479). In the 6th chapel is a wooden *Crucifix* of the 15th cent. The altar at one transept end has a modern canvas by the Dominican P. Spinillo between two Baroque, stucco statues of *Magdalene* and *St. Catherine of Alexandria*. The big monument to engineer *Giuseppe Pianigiani* who planned the Siena - Empoli railway is by Enea Becheroni (1858) and was finished by Tito Sarrocchi. Remains of decorative frescoes of the 14th cent. have been discovered on the left wall of the nave. On the

Saint's Head (as is known, her body is buried in S. Maria della Minerva in Rome), which can be seen behind a screen in the middle of a beautiful marble altar by Giovanni di Stefano (1469). The altar is flanked by two famous frescoes, the Saint's *Swoon* and *Ecstasy* by Sodoma (1526), also the author of the crowded *Beheading of Niccolò di Tuldo assisted by the Saint* on the left wall and the powerful figures of *St. Jerome* and St. Luke (?) on the arch underside. Below are the images of the two biographers of the Saint, *Blessed Raimon-*

do of Capua and *Blessed Tommaso Nacci*, oil frescoes by Francesco Vanni (1593-96) who, with the same technique, painted the *Healing of a possessed woman* on the right wall. The graffito floor is a very valuable art work with *Orpheus taming a wild beast* probably by Giovanni di Stefano. Back to the church we see, under an arch with Angels' heads, fragments of a fresco by Paolo di Giovanni Fei, a fresco coming from a pilaster of the left wall representing the *Virgin and Child blessing a warrior introduced to him by the Baptist* by Pietro Lorenzetti.

Basilica of San Domenico: 1. Overall view of the Basilica; 2. The wide nave; 3. The Chapel of Santa Caterina, almost completely frescoed by Sodoma.

Through Piazza S. Domenico and Viale dei Mille, passing along the Municipal Stadium, we reach an open space with a bronze statue of *St. Catherine*, a recent work by Brunetto Buracchini behind which are the powerful bastions of the *Fort of S. Barbara* built by Cosimo I de' Medici after a plan by Baldassarre Lanci from Urbino (1560), with a quadrilateral base and massive angular bulwarks. The bastions, which form a walkway, limit a wide area called Piazza della Libertà. Through Viale 25 Aprile we reach the LIZZA (to its left is the entrance to the Fort having, under a bastion, the ENOTECA ITALICA PERMANENTE, Italian standing stock of vintage wines for the exhibition, tasting and sale of wines), a large public garden set up in 1779 with an equestrian statue of *Giuseppe Garibaldi* by Raffaello Romanelli (1896). Viale Cesare Maccari, running by the Lizza, ends into Piazza Gramsci at one end of which is the CHURCH OF S. STEFANO ALLA LIZZA, rebuilt in 1641 and having over the high altar a big *polyptych* by Andrea Vanni (1400) with a beautiful predella (*Crucifixion and stories of St. Stephen*) by Giovanni di Paolo. Beyond the large Piazza Gramsci and the palace of the Chamber of Commerce is Piazza Matteotti, where the CENTRAL POST OFFICE by Vittorio Mariani stands (1912); then we turn left into Via dei Montanini where we reach the isolated ORATORY OF S. MARIA DELLE NEVI, an elegant Renaissance construction after a plan attributed to Francesco di Giorgio Martini (1471) which contains a big altar piece of the *Madonna of the Snow*, a masterpiece by Matteo di Giovanni (1477). Further along Via dei Montanini we come to the Romanesque *Church of S. Andrea*, to the right, where we can see over its high altar a *Crowning of the Virgin between St. Peter and Andrea*, a triptych by Giovanni di Paolo (1445). Beyond Via Garibaldi, Via dei Montanini continues into Via Camollia where the Arch of Fontegiusta leads down to the church of S. MARIA IN PORTICO A FONTEGIUSTA built in 1482-84 after a plan by Francesco Fedeli and Giacomo di Giovanni da Como. The architrave of the portal bears an image of the *Virgin among Angels* attributed to Giovanni di Stefano (1489). The beautiful and original interior has a square plan with a nave and two aisles covered by vaults of the same height: the oculus on the façade encloses a stained-glass window by Guidoccio Cozzarelli, surrounded by weapons, collected by the Sienese at the battle of Poggio Imperiale, and by the shoulder-bone of a whale allegedly donated by Cristoforo Colom-

first altar is a *Virgin with Child* by Francesco Vannuccio (Ca.1370) inside a big panel painting with the *Everlasting and 4 Saints* by Sodoma and a 15-panel predella from the 16th century. Then there are three more canvases: *St. Anthony Abbot freeing a possessed woman* by Rutilio Manetti (1628), *Mystical wedding of St. Catherine of Alexandria* by Sebastiano Folli and *St. Giacinto saving a statue of the Virgin from a fire* by Francesco Vanni (1600). Four stained-glass windows representing the Saint have so far been carried out, by Bruno Saetti and Domenico Cantatore to the right and Fabrizio Clerici and Giorgio Quaroni to

the left. A stairway leads down to the crypt, a suggestive early 14th-century area with a nave and two aisles, corresponding to the overlying transept and overlooked by a huge *Painted cross* by Sano di Pietro (Ca.1460). On the walls are some canvases of the 17th and 18th cent. among which, in the left apse, a *Crucifixion* by Ventura Salimbeni. Outside the main entrance to the crypt, the imposing architectonic structures of the transept can be admired and also a charming view of a section of the town is offered, with the marble mass of the Duomo overlooking multicoloured houses and vegetable gardens in Vallepi-

bo who, according to tradition, lived in Siena as a student where he fell in love with a girl from Camollia. On the arch to the right of the entrance is located a *Visitation*, fresco by Michelangelo Anselmi: in a corner is a small bronze ciborium attributed to Giovanni da Zagabria called «delle Bombarde», the father of the painter Girolamo del Pacchia, who died in 1479. Over the altars of the right wall, *Jesus, Mary and two Saints* by Francesco Vanni and *Crowning of the Virgin* by Bernardino Fungai; the choir dates back to the year 1500. The high altar is a refined work by Lorenzo Marrina, helped by Michele Cioli from Settignano who carried out the *Pietà* in the lunette: on the altar is a *Virgin with Child*, a peeled-off fresco of the 14th century. In the overlying big lunette, we can see the *Assumption*, a fresco by Girolamo di Benvenuto (1515). Beside the lateral door is a bronze holy-water stoup by Giovanni di Zagabria (1430), then *Sybil announcing the birth of the Redeemer to Augustus*, important fresco painted by Baldassarre Peruzzi when he returned to Siena after the sack of Rome (1527). Moreover: *St. Sebastian*, a wooden statue by Giovanni di Stefano and, right of the entrance, the *Plague of Siena* by Bartolomeo Neroni called «Riccio».

Via Camollia, along which, to the left, is the Romanesque CHURCH OF S. PIETRO ALLA MAGIONE, formerly Church of the Templars and later of the Knights of Malta, ends at **Porta Camollia**, a gate rebuilt in 1604 after a plan by Alessandro Casolani having on an external arch a famous writing in honour of Ferdinando I de' Medici, now a sign of welcome to town visitors: «Cor magis tibi Sena pandit» (Siena opens to you its gate and even more its heart). Outside the gate is Viale Vittorio Emanuele where, to the left, is a column reminding of Frederick III meeting his betrothed Eleonora of Portugal (the event was depicted by Pinturicchio on the best fresco of the Piccolomini Library), and the avenue finally reaches the powerful ANTIPORTO OF CAMOLLIA (outpost) of the 14th cent., the farthest defence post to the north of Siena.

About 1 km. from here is the PALAZZO DEI DIAVOLI (formerly Palazzo dei Turchi), a peculiar building by Antonio Federighi (1460), flanked by a chapel and a cylindric tower.

4

5

6

Basilica of San Domenico: 1. St. Catherine intercedes on the salvation of the soul of a tortured man, by Sodoma; 2. Portrait of the Saint, fresco by Andrea Vanni; 3. Faint of the Saint, by Sodoma; 4. Northern walls of the Fortress with emblem of the Medici family, built in 1560 for Cosimo I; 5. The Lizza with monument of G. Garibaldi; 6. Porta Camollia.

THE PALIO

The Palio delle Contrade (the town's districts) is undoubtedly the most famous, most beautiful and most deeply loved among Italy's popular festivals. It combines and brings to their highest signification the features of a religious and of a civil holiday, of a charming show and of a historical commemoration, which culminate in a frenzied horse race where the pride and the fervent competitive spirit of the town districts are exalted. The Contrade are in fact peculiar institutions whose origin dates back to the 15th century and which correspond today to the seventeen districts into which Siena is divided, according to a regulation issued on 7 January 1730 by Violante of Bavaria, the governor of Siena. Each Contrada has its own seat, a church (separated and indipendent from the parish church), a museum holding the Palii (banners) which have been won and old and recent mementoes. It is governed by a «Seggio» (board) elected by the people, presided over by a Prior and helped by a Captain, who is given full powers about the organization of the race. The Contrade of the three parts of the town (the so-called terzi) are marked by their badges and colours as follows: TERZO OF TOWN: AQUILA (two-headed, crowned eagle - yellow with black and deep blue stripes) - CHIOCCIOLA (snail - yellow and red with deep blue stripes) - ONDA, the Wave (crowned dolphin - white and light blue) - PANTERA (rampant panther - red and deep blue with yellow stripes) - SELVA, the Woods (rhinoceros under an oak - green and orange with yellow stripes) - TARTUCA (tortoise - yellow and deep blue). TERZO OF S. MARTINO: CIVETTA (owl - black and red with white stripes) - LEOCORNO (unicorn - white and orange

with deep blue stripes) - NICCHIO (crowned shell - deep blue with yellow and red stripes) - TORRE, the Tower (elephant with a tower on its back - amaranth with white and deep blue stripes) - VALDIMONTONE (ram - white and yellow with red stripes). TERZO OF CAMOLLIA: BRUCO (grub - yellow and green with deep blue stripes) - DRAGO (winged dragon - red and green with yellow stripes) - GIRAFFA (giraffe - white and red) - ISTRICE (porcupine - white with black, red and deep blue stripes) - LUPA (Roman she-wolf - white and black with orange stripes) - OCA (crowned goose - white and green with red stripes). Ten of the seventeen Contrade run by turns on the square to contend for the Palio, which is a silk banner with historical, allegorical or religious figures painted in most cases by artists of great, often international renown. The race is run twice a year, on 2 July, in

honour of the Madonna of Provenzano, and on 16 August, in honour of the Our Lady of the Assumption, patron saint of Siena, on the piazza del Campo (Campo square), whose «ring», around the paved portion of the square, is turned into a race track by means of a thick layer of yellow earth, or «tuff», and is surrounded on either sides by tiers of seats and barriers. The race, or «carriera», is preceded by parades carried out according to an almost ritualistic programme. In the morning of 29 June and on 13 August the «tratta» takes place, that is the drawing of lots of the ten contrade and the distribution of the horses which have been chosen by a specially designed commission out of 20 or 30, after proving fit for the race through «heat» racing. During that same day and the following ones, six trials are run, the last of which, on the morning of the feast day, is called «la provaccia» (a badly run trial), because

the horses' strength is saved for the imminent contest. On the evening before the race a great «propitiatory dinner» is organized by the town quarters taking part in the competition, and, the next day at 3 p.m., the big bell of the Town Hall tower calls the contrade together. Each of them provides for the blessing of its horse in its own church and for the clothing of the «comparse», that is those present at the historical parade: this is formed by about 800 people wearing charming costumes inspired mostly by the imaginative and magnificent dresses seen in 15th-century paintings, and creates a spectacular and orderly choreography of exceptional beauty. The procession enters the square through the «bocca di Casato» and is opened by 6 «mazzieri» (mace-bearers) and by the white and black banner of the Municipality escorted by «comandatori». 18 buglers follow with silver «clarions» together with 30 «musici di palazzo» (palace musicians), and then the standard-bearers and the representatives of the Landed gentry, the Podestà and Vicariates, representing the estates of the ancient Sienese State, the People's Captain and the Gonfaloniers of the Terzi of the Town, with their mounted retinues, a group symbolizing the University, a standard-bearer and three Magistrates of the Trade Court with a crowded group of representatives of the Guilds, and finally a pageboy bearing the «masgalano» (a silver

1. The Campo during the Palio «mass»; 2. One of the chiefs of the Palio parade.

prize for the best «comparsa» of the
Campo). After this procession come the
«comparse» of the 10 Contrade which
run the Palio, each of them being formed
by about 15 people, among whom are to
be seen the «duce» (the chief) on foot,
two «alfieri» (standard-bearers),
drummer-boys, soldiers and standard-
bearers, the jockey, on a parade-horse
called «soprallasso» and the race-horse,
called «barbero», of which the «bar-
baresco» holds the reins: a double row
of pageboys with laurel garlands pre-
cedes the «comparse» of the 7 contrade
which do not take part in the race (which
therefore have no barbero), and knights
who symbolize 6 suppressed Contrade
(GALLO-ROOSTER, LEONE-LION, ORSO-
BEAR, VIPERA-VIPER and SPADAFORTE-
SWORD), followed by the Justice Captain
on horseback with his footman: he advances together with a crowded escort of
crossbowmen, «pavesari» (flag-bearers),
foot-soldiers, followed by the ornamented «carroccio» (cart), pulled by two couples of oxen, on which are the Palio, the
pennon of the Municipality, six small
trumpets and the Four Members of the
Balia, and he rings continually a small
bell called «martinella». At the end of
the procession are six knights with foot-
men, representing the noble families of
the Town and a row of pageboys with
laurel garlands. The procession advances
slowly, stopping now and then to allow
the standard bearers of the Contrade to
wave and throw the flags in the air, an
ancient game, called «sbandierata»
which creates complicated and very ele-

Images from the Palio historical parade and the race.

gant figures of virtuosity between couples (among which are the «passaggio di collo», neck passage, the «salto di fiocco», bow jump, and the exchange of flags «per alzata», by tossing) whose rhythm is marked by the beating of drums. Once the «comparse» of the procession are sitting on the tiers of the lower part of the square, the bearers of all the Contrade perform, with perfect synchronism, the last flag waving before the Public Palace. The race consists of three laps, start and finishing line being in front of the tier of the judges where the Palio is waving. The horses are lined up between two «canapi» (ropes) according to an order which is kept secret until the last minute, and, usually after several false starts caused by the animals' restlessness, the ropes are lowered by a

«mossiere», the starter, and, at the simultaneous bang of a firework, the race begins. The jockeys, highly skilful and reckless riders bearing the colours of the Contrada which has engaged them, ride bare-back, prodding on their horses with a lash. The three laps are run at frantic speed and usually during the race a number of dramatic episodes occur, often horses fall (at the steep bend of S. Martino, protected by mattresses) amid the roaring of a crowd which totals about 70 thousand people thronging the square and the tiers or looking out of adorned windows. Immediately after the end of this very hard-fought race the silk cloth is handed to the exulting citizens of the winning Contrada, who will bear it in triumph for some days along the town streets, and the feast ends with a grandi-

ose dinner on the main street or square of the Contrada, transformed by a fantastic scenography. Although the Palio, which represents the soul of Siena itself, is not a show specially organized for tourists, these are friendly welcomed in the Contrade, where they inevitably sympathize with the passion of their inhabitants.

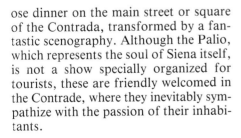

The Palio race: cheerful processions and dinner in the victorious contrada.

BASILICA DELL'OSSERVANZA -
It rises on Capriola hill at about 3 km.
from Porta Ovile and it was built on an
old hermitage donated to St. Bernardino by the Spedale in 1404. The present
church was erected from 1474 to 1518 after a plan which is now attributed to
Francesco di Giorgio Martini, later
replaced by Giacomo Cozzarelli. Its lu-
minuous interior with one nave flanked
by chapels and with a dome is one of the
most beautiful examples of Sienese
Renaissance architecture (after being destroyed in 1944 by an air raid, it was
rebuilt with the same form and material). On the rearfaçade wall can be seen
St. Bonaventura and *St. Ludovico from
Toulouse*, tondos of glazed terra-cotta by
Andrea della Robbia and, on both sides
of the presbytery's arch, the *Annunciation* statues by the same author (ca.1485);
in the 1st chapel to the right, *Crucifixion and Saints*, a peeled-off fresco by
Bartolomeo Neroni called «Riccio»
(1549). In the 2nd one there is the
Mourning over dead Jesus, a terra-cotta
group formerly ascribed to «Cieco da
Gambassi» (early 17th cent.) but actually by an unidentified Tuscan sculptor
from the mid-16th cent. (perhaps
Giovanni di Paolo Neri). In the 3rd one
*Virgin with Child between St. Jerome
and Bernardino* by Sano di Pietro (1463),
St. Bernardino by Pietro di Giovanni
d'Ambrogio (dated 1444, when the Saint
died) and *St. Elizabeth of Hungary* by
Girolamo di Benvenuto. In the 4th
St. Virgin Ambrose and Jerome, with Child
altar piece dated 1336 after which the «Maestro dell'Osservanza», a contemporary of
Sassetta, was named. In the choir *Virgin
with Child and St. John the Baptist and
Jerome*, a peeled-off fresco with corresponding sinopite, attributed to Pietro
degli Orioli. In the 1st chapel to the left
Virgin with Child by Sano di Pietro. In
the 2nd one, *Crowning of the Virgin and
Saints*, altar piece of glazed terra-cotta
by Andrea della Robbia (the Madonna's
bust is a copy from a photograph of the
original one destroyed in the 1944 bombing). In the 3rd one, *Crucifixion* by Riccio and, in the 4th one, *Four Saints*, parts
of a polyptych by Andrea di Bartolo
(1413). We pass then into the sacristy
where a *Mourning over dead Jesus* can
be seen, a group of coloured terra-cotta
rightly considered the masterpiece of
Giacomo Cozzarelli (ca.1497). Beside the
sacristy is the small *Museum Aurelio
Castelli* where the fragmented head of a
wooden Crucifix, formerly on the high
altar of the church, can be seen. When
the crucifix was destroyed by the war a
parchment was found inside the head
with a moving prayer written by Lando
di Pietro who sculptured it in 1338; more

The surrounding areas

*Basilica dell'Osservanza • Pontificio Seminario Regionale • Castle of Bel-
caro • Castle of the Four Towers • The Charterhouse of Pontignano • Hermitages of Lecceto and S. Leonardo al Lago • Pieve di Ponte allo Spino*

objects are a *Reliquiary for St. Bernardino's tunic*, made of silver, by Francesco
d'Antonio (1461), a peeled-off fresco of
the *Last Judgement* by Girolamo di Benvenuto (ca.1500) and a rich series of
miniated codices among which is a *De
Animalibus* by Albertus Magnus with il-
lustrations by Francesco di Giorgio Martini, 12 choir-books by masters of the
15th cent. and other books, vestments
and goldsmith's pieces.

**PONTIFICIO SEMINARIO
REGIONALE** in Montarioso, along the
Via Chiantigiana. Several of the important works of art collected here will be
moved to a Diocesan Museum, presently under construction. Some of them are:

Virgin with Child and Stories coming
from the church of Tressa, after which
the «Maestro di Tressa» was named (early 13th cent.); *Virgin with Child*, a small
stained-glass window coming from the
church of the Grotta, by the school of
Guido da Siena (mid-13th cent.); two
Virgins with Child by Segna di Bonaventura; *Assumption* from Terrensano, of
the school of Duccio; *Resurrected Christ*,
fresco peeled off from the cloister of S.
Francesco, a masterpiece by Pietro
Lorenzetti; *Virgin of Milk*, coming from
the Seminar, a masterpiece by Ambro-

*1. Basilica dell'Osservanza; 2. Pontificio Semina-
rio Regionale: Virgin of Milk, masterpiece by Ambrogio Lorenzetti.*

gio Lorenzetti; *Virgin with Child* from the church of S. Pietro a Ovile after which the «Maestro d'Ovile» was named, a painter of the group of Pietro Lorenzetti who is now identified by many as Bartolomeo Bulgarini; *Virgin with Child* by Naddo Ceccarelli; *Mourning over dead Jesus*, fresco peeled off from the cloister of S. Francesco by Lorenzo di Pietro called «Vecchietta»; *Virgin with Child* from the house of the canons of S. Ansano in Dofana, attributed to Baldassarre Peruzzi; *Virgin with Child* by Girolamo di Benvenuto; three-panel predella of the school of Giovanni di Paolo and several canvases by Alessandro Casolani and Ventura Salimbeni. Among the sculptures: *St. Paul*, a small polychrome wood statue painted by Stefano alla Lizza and attributed to Domenico di Niccolò dei Cori, and *Virgin with Child*, a marble relief from the cloister of S. Francesco, attributed to Antonio Federighi. Among the goldsmith's objects: *Procession cross* of the 13th-cent. Rhine school; *Reliquiary of St. Galgano* formerly in the abbey of S. Galgano and later in the house of the canons of Frosini, attributed to Viva di Lando (ca.1330); then an *Antiphonary for the feast of St. Mary Magdalene* with miniatures by Lippo Vanni (ca.1345).

CASTLE OF BELCARO - An old fortress (1199) about 7 km. outside Porta S. Marco, it was turned into a villa by Baldassarre Peruzzi who frescoed a *Paris' judgement* on its vestibule, a *Virgin with Saints* and *Stories of Martyrs* on the apse of the chapel and *Mythological episodes* with foilage decorations on the loggia ceiling (ca.1535, many times restored).

CASTLE OF THE FOUR TOWERS - About 9.5 km. outside Porta Pispini, this grandiose and slender quadrilateral building has four towers at its corners (one being smaller than the others) mentioned since the middle of the 13th but probably built in the 14th cent. (now a private house with a typical courtyard).

CERTOSA OF PONTIGNANO - It lies at 8 km. outside Porta Ovile and was founded in 1348 by Bindo Petroni (today Collegio Universitario «M.Bracci», a boarding-school). The Charterhouse has three cloisters: the first of the 16th cent., the second, which is smaller, of the 14th cent. and the third, very large and surrounded by the former monk cells, of the 15th century. In the former refectory we can see the *Last supper*, a fresco by Bernardino Poccetti (1596) also the author of a *St. Brunone's death* in the big cloister. The church, consecrated in 1606 is really brimming with works in the Florentine late Mannerist taste: its vaults are in fact frescoed by Poccetti (with *Sto-*

2

ries of the Baptist and the Virgin) and its walls with *Stories of St. Peter and St. Paul*, by Poccetti, his follower Orazio Porta, Giovanni Battista Brugieri and by brother Stefano Cassiani. The choir seats are by Domenico Atticciati. In the adjoining big chapel, *Crucifixion* by Francesco Vanni and frescoes by Giuseppe Nasini (18th cent.) are to be seen.

HERMITAGES OF LECCETO AND S. LEONARDO AL LAGO - It is advisable to visit these hermitages, both Augustinian ones and at the same distance from Siena (9 km.), during the same tour passing through Porta S. Marco and, at Colonna di S. Marco, following Via Montalbuccio until the bridge over the Rigo stream: there, on the left along the road of Ferratore, a carriageway goes up to LECCETO, a fortress-hermitage overlooked by a massive tower. According to tradition it was founded in the 4th cent.

but it was built during the 14th and 15th century. On the arcade in front of the church, we can see a lunette with the *Redeemer* attributed to Paolo di Neri, a follower of Pietro Lorenzetti and frescoes representing *Heaven, Hell, Human life in peace and at war*, the *Sacraments* and *Works of Mercy* of the early 15th cent. by at least two different authors, one of whom shows influences of the late northern Gothic style. In the two adjoining cloisters are significant Sienese frescoes made of green earth material with *Episodes of life at the hermitage*, some of which ascribed to Pietro di Giovanni d'Ambrogio (1442) and others, with less probability, to Carlo di Giovanni.

Beyond the bridge on the Rigo, to the right along a flat road and then turning left into a cart-track, we reach S. LEONARDO AL LAGO, in the middle of a forest, with a beautiful 14th-century

church. Inside the church, over a big arch of the choir, is *Our Lady of the Assumption*; on piers *St. Leonard, St. Augustine* and *St. Augustine with St. Monica*; in the choir, on the vaulting cells, *Playing angels* and, on the walls, *Annunciation, Presentation into the temple* and *Virgin's wedding*, masterpieces by Lippo Vanni (ca.1360-1370), showing brilliant perspective solutions derived from Pietro Lorenzetti.

PIEVE DI PONTE ALLO SPINO - Outside Porta S. Marco, going on the Statale (trunk road) 73, we turn right after *Costalpino* (5 km.) and at *Volte Basse* (after 900 mt. to the left is *Villa delle Volte* commissioned by Sigismondo Chigi in 1505 after a plan by Baldassarre Peruzzi) we turn right again. At km 10.6 to the left is the beautiful *Pieve di S. Giovanni Battista* in Ponte allo Spino, of the 12th cent., which was granted in 1189 to the bishop of Siena by Clement III. It is one of the most interesting Romanesque buildings on the Sienese territory, with a nave and two aisles, all of them rather slender and divided by cross-shaped pillars with capitals decorated with figures and wicker-typed intertwining, a high square lantern and three apses. Beside the façade is a square bell tower with one and two-light mullioned windows and, on the right side are the remains of a cloister and the rectory with three Gothic two-light mullioned windows.

Inside the parish church with a Neogothic façade is a canvas - *Madonna with 4 Saints* - attrib. to Alessandro Casolani. Continuing on the same road, about 3 km. ahead, we turn left in the direction of ANCAIANO in which is a beautiful church, commissioned in 1662 by Alexander VII, with inside a *Madonna* of the 14th cent. and two panel paintings of the school of Riccio. CENTINALE, a wonderful villa rising at 2 km. from here, was commissioned by Card. Flavio Chigi in 1680 after a plan by Carlo Fontana: its large woods, called «Thebaid» are dotted with chapels and with monster-like figures sculptured by Bartolomeo Mazzuoli, also the author of a relief representing the visit of Grand Duke Cosimo III to the villa. In front of the gate a picturesque slope leads to a hermitage where the Cardinal used to go for penance.

1. Castle of Belcaro; 2. Castle of the Four Towers; 3. Hermitage of Lecceto.
1. Panoramic view of Monteriggioni, surrounded by its towered walls of the 13th cent.

MONTERIGGIONI

Coming along Via Cavour and through Porta Camollia we follow for about 10 km. the Via Cassia until we reach **Monteriggioni** which stands on top of a hill, encompassed by the circular boundary of its 13th-century walls with 14 quadrangular towers: 7 of them have been recently raised, even if they must have been much higher, since Dante compared them to the giants in Hell («come su la cerchia tonda - Monteriggion di torri si corona», *Inferno* XXXI, 41-42). The village, made of small houses alternating with vegetable gardens, has a parish church of the early 14th century. Further along the Via Cassia, at 5 km. from here, we pass through STAGGIA, a village fortified by the Florentine during the 14th century and overlooked by a massive castle-keep from the first half of the 15th cent. with two large cylindrical towers and another high tower. Inside the PIEVE OF S. MARIA ASSUNTA, restored in romanesque forms, is a panel painting with *Virgin and Child* of 14th. cent. Sienese school, remains of frescoes of the same century and a small stained-glass window with *Magdalene* of the 15th cent. (a panel painting with the *Communion of Magdalene* by Antonio del Pollaiolo has been recently moved to the Cathedral of Colle Val d'Elsa).

POGGIBONSI

Another 5 km. ahead, the Via Cassia goes through **Poggibonsi**, an import ant small village built on the Borgo Marturi flat under the fort of PODIUM BONITII, the object of several disputes between the Sienese and the Florentine and destroyed in 1270 by Guido di Monforte, now the largest industrial centre in the province of Siena. In the CHURCH OF S. LORENZO, a wooden *Crucifix* attributed to Giovanni d'Agostino and a *St. Nicolò from Tolentino*, panel painting by Neri di Bicci. The *Palazzo Pretorio* retains some of its Gothic elements; it is flanked by a medieval tower and several coats of arms can be seen on its façade. The COLLEGIATA (collegiate church), rebuilt in 1860, still has a bell tower which was once a tower of the old castle of Marturi: inside the church are a *baptismal font* of 1341 and, in the apse, a *Resurrection* attrib. to Vincenzo Tamagni (16th cent.).

SAN GIMIGNANO

12 km. away from Poggibonsi is **San Gimignano**, a charming small town (at 330 mt.) with slender towers rising on a

ROUTES IN THE PROVINCE OF SIENA

Montereggioni • S. Gimignano • S. Quirico D'Orcia • Montalcino • Monte Amiata • Monte Oliveto Maggiore • Pienza • Montepulciano • Chianciano

4

hill which overlooks a verdant landscape.

A number of archaeological finds - tombs and various furnishings - in today's town centre or in the surrounding areas - testify of its being originally an Etruscan site, though the name of St. Gimignano was first mentioned in the 10th century: he was the Bishop of Modena who, according to tradition (although with no evidence from historical records), freed by the Barbarians the legendary village of SILVIA in the 5th century. Around 1100 the village became a City-State with its own consuls and, after long struggles against nearby towns, especially Volterra, as well as constant internecine war between the two powerful families of the Guelph Ardinghelli and the Ghibelline Salvucci, passed under the complete control of Florence in 1353 and from then on had no history of its own. The first inhabited settlement lay between a castle, from time to time the seat of the bishop of Volterra or of his delegate, and the area of Montestaffoli, formerly belonging to the Langobard Astulfulo («Mons Astulfuli») and, during the 12th cent., it was encompassed by walls. Then, from the second half of the 12th to the whole 13th cent., along the Francigena or Romean Way (the most important medieval artery leading from Rome

to the Cisa pass and then to northern Europe) the suburbs of S. Giovanni and S. Matteo were raised, surrounded in 1262 by a new wall boundary of 2,176 mt. The town of S. Gimignano mainly retains an artistic interest, both because its street layout and architectural elements from the 13th cent. have remained almost unchanged since then, thus forming a unique example in the whole of Italy, and also for the immense wealth of paintings and sculptures in its churches and museums, some of which of extraordinary importance. A typical feature characterizing the town are its towers of the 12th, 13th and 14th century, once used as houses, defence posts and as the symbol of power and pride of the City-State and of the aristocratic families who built them. Originally totalling 72 and now only 15, they have made the town well-known as «beautifully-towered S. Gimignano». The artistic works in the town are closely related to its historical events, so that buildings in the 13th and 14th cent. show themes of Pisan, Sienese and Florentine origin, while almost all the paintings in the 14th cent. show Sienese inspiration and 15th-and 16th-century art is influenced by Florence.

A visit to the town starts usually from the tree-lined Piazza Martiri di Monte-

blic building of the town and formerly a private possession where the Podesta lived paying a rent (the palace was then bought by the Commune in 1320); beside it is a high tower called «LA ROGNOSA» (51 mt.): on the underlying big vault is a damaged fresco by Sodoma. The interior was turned into a theatre in the 16th cent., then rebuilt in the 18th century and it is presently being restructured. On the left side is PALAZZO DEL POPOLO, before which are the TWIN TOWERS of the Salvucci family.

PALAZZO DEL POPOLO or PALAZZO NUOVO DEL PODESTÀ - The seat of the Town Hall, attributed without proof to Arnolfo di Cambio, this building was begun in the 8th-9th decade of the 13th cent. and in 1300 the TORRE GROSSA was also initiated: it was ended in 1311 by a Maestro Tinuccio and it reached a height of 54 mt., a height which private towers were not allowed to pass. A first nucleus, made of a hall on a two-aisled room on the ground floor, later divided into two floors, was enlarged in depth in 1323, thereby adding a loggia which was later walled up in part. The building of an isolated body at the back produced a «claustrum palatii» with a loggia and a hanging outside stair. The façade, several times restructured, is made of stone on the ground floor, with three Sienese arches, and of bricks on the two upper floors, with Florentine depressed arched windows, probably of the 15th cent.: the jutting embattlement on small hanging arches was added in 1881 by Giuseppe Partini. To the right, on top of two flights of stairs, is the «arringo» where the Podesta took the oath of loyalty to the statutes: on 19 August 1362, Rossellino and Primerano Ardinghelli and Agnolo Bartali, unjustly accused of treachery, were beheaded on instigation of the Salvucci family at the foot of the building. To the left a loggia was built in 1338, reopened in 1933, under which a frescoed lunette was placed with the Virgin between *St. Michael Archangel and the Baptist* from the 14th cent., coming from a demolished chapel behind the Founts.

We enter the picturesque courtyard with a 1361 tank and several coat of arms of podestas painted on the walls. On the right is the Loggia del Giudice (Judge's loggia) where justice was administered and frescoes are related to that theme: a *Virgin with Child between St. Gimignano and St. Gregory* (Jesus is showing the warning «Diligite Justitiam qui judicatis

maggio from which part of the town walls can be seen, with one of the circular bastions commissioned by Cosimo I de' Medici. We enter through the 13th-century PORTA S. GIOVANNI, overlooked by a guardhouse and with the two remaining aisles of the CHURCH OF THE MADONNA DEI LUMI built inside the gate in 1601, whose nave was demolished in 1928 to make the passage easier. Via S. Giovanni goes up among medieval houses, some of which are typical tower-houses, and then we pass by the remains of the façade of the CHURCH OF S. FRANCESCO, in Pisan Romanesque style; further ahead, to the left, is the 14th-century PRATELLESI PALACE, with a beautiful façade of bricks with two-light mullioned windows, the seat of the Municipal Library and Historical Archives, in whose hall is a fresco by Vincenzo Tamagni from S. Gimignano representing the *Mystical wedding of St. Catherine of Ale-*

xandria (1528). At the end of the street is the ARCH OF THE BECCI opened in the oldest circle of walls, through which we enter the triangular Piazza della Cisterna, built in 1273 with puteal and architraved columns from 1346. It is surrounded by buildings dating back mostly to the 14th cent., among which, to the right, TORTOLI PALACE with two orders of two-light mullioned windows, in front of which stands the TORRE DEL DIAVOLO (Devil tower, so called because its owner, returning from a journey, found it higher than it was when he had left, and considered this a devil's work). To the left are the 13th-cent. TWIN TOWERS of the Ardinghelli family.

Beside the Piazza della Cisterna is the Piazza del Duomo, which retains an extremely picturesque medieval character. In front of the Cathedral stairway is the 13th-cent. PALAZZO ANTICO DEL PODESTÀ, wrongly considered the oldest pu-

S. Gimignano: 1. Panoramic view; 2. Piazza della Cisterna; 3. Courtyard of Palazzo del Popolo (1288).

terram») by a Sienese author close to Lippo Vanni (2nd half of the 14th cent.), *St. Ivo Patron of lawyers* obtaining justice in his court by Sodoma with the collaboration of Vincenzo Tamagni (1507) and a *Magistrate* who, together with Prudence and Truth, is trampling upon Lie: on the painting, above, is the writing: «Per quel che pecha l'uom per quel patisce - cava la verità a la bugia - la falsa lingua qual sempre mentisce» (Man is punished according to his sins - and truth is to be drawn from lie - as false tongues are bound to lie). Through an external stair we go up to the second floor where, on the right, is the hall of the Council, called «Dante's Hall» as the poet spoke here on 8 May 1300 in favour of the constitution of a Guelph league in Tuscany. On the wall opposite the window is a big fresco of the «*Maestà*»: the Virgin on the throne with Child among Angels and 14 Saints and Podesta Nello di Mino de' Tolomei on his knees before them. It is a work by Lippo Memmi who signed under the Virgin while an inscription on the frame reports the name of the client and the date 1317. On the step to the right is the writing: BENOZUS FLORENTINUS PICTOR RESTAURAVIT ANNO DOMINI MCCCCLXVII (1467). Also the two couples of Saints at the right and left end are attributed to Gozzoli, but the scene was probably enlarged in the 2nd half of the 14th cent., perhaps by Bartolo di Fredi and it is also probable that Gozzoli only modified the heads of the Saints Bartolo and Luigi IX, repainted the blue background and re-gilded the Virgin's throne. The scene, which showed better proportions in its original version, where the two young Saints were standing at both sides supporting the poles of the silken canopy, was clearly inspired by the famous *Maestà* by Simone Martini painted two years before (1315) in the Sienese Palazzo Pubblico. Although the stiff arrangement of figures in the foreground of this work, which is the first attributable to Lippo Memmi with certainty, lacks the animated airiness and space depth of its inspirer, the young painter, who would later become the brother-in-law and closest collaborator of Martini in 1324, proves here to be a highly refined master both in colours and in the soft flesh-pink of the beautiful faces, at the same time adding to the celestial gathering a lively touch of contemporary flavour through the beautiful portrait of Tolomei. On the opposite wall are badly damaged hunting and tournament scenes and, on the end wall, *The inhabitants of S. Gimignano taking their oath of loyalty to King Charles of Anjou*, painted before 1293, probably attrib. to a painter Azzo, still sho-

2

3

wing Byzantine influences and reminding of Cimabue and Coppo di Marcovaldo. On the spot where the Gonfalonier of Justice was, is a writing which warns: «Preposto - odi benigno ciascun che propone - rispondi gratioso et fa ragione» (Delegate - listen kindly to anyone's proposal - answer with grace and act rightly).

Beside the hall is a room for secret gatherings with benches and «bigoncia» (pulpit) for the speaker from 1475 and a 16th-cent. bust of *St. Bartholomew*; in the adjoining room, where a collection of ceramics of the Spedale of S. Fina was exhibited (now moved to S. Lorenzo in Ponte while its definitive seat in the former convent of S. Chiara is being set up), the terra-cotta bust considered the portrait of the hospital director Guido Marabottini (d. 1256) is a sharply realistic

work by a Florentine sculptor of the end of the 15th century.

Going upstairs, after one flight, we enter to the left the former chapel of the Podesta with a fresco representing *Trinity* and 6 small stories from 1497 attrib. to Pier Francesco Fiorentino, follower of Gozzoli, a panel painting with *Virgin between St. Giusto and Clemente* by the same author (1477) and a *Christ's pietà* a peeled-off fresco by the same author (1497), a panel painting with *Christ's pietà and busts of figures of the Passion* by a Florentine close to Neri di Bicci, a small detached fresco with *Crucifix adored by St. Jerome, St. Francis and a devout* by Benozzo Gozzoli with a collaborator and an altar-piece with a *Virgin with Child and 5 Saints* attrib. to Leonardo Malatesta from Pistoia (16th cent.).

S. Gimignano: 1. Twin towers of the Salvucci family; 2. A street in the town centre; 3. Medieval tower and Becci arch; 4. The Cathedral or Collegiate Church of S. Maria Assunta; 5. Interior.

4

THE CATHEDRAL, or COLLEGIA-TE CHURCH OF S. MARIA ASSUN-TA,

stands on a higher level than the square's, to which it is connected by a stairway from 1264, changed in 1493 and rebuilt in 1701. The Cathedral, or Duomo, was built on the area where an oratory from the 9th or 10th cent. stood, inversely oriented if compared to the present church, and was consecrated in 1148 by Pope Eugenio III. Its façade, at which a Maestro Brunisemd, perhaps a Lombard, worked in 1239, has two entrance doors corresponding to the aisles, instead of a central portal: on one side of the front, on an arch through which we pass into Piazza Pecori, is a statue of *S. Gimignano* which, in 1342, was placed over Porta alle Fonti in memory of the vain attempt of the exiles of S. Gimignano to seize power. The longitudinal structure inside the cathedral is Romanesque in style and has a double row of monolithic columns with sober capitals supporting seven wide round arches: the nave was raised in the early 14th cent. and covered with Gothic cross-vaults; the walls of the clerestory have monochrome paintings with small angels bearing garlands and medaillons with busts of *Apostles* carried out in 1474-75 by Pier Francesco Fiorentino to whom the *Christ's pietà* on the presbyterial arch is also attributed.

In 1466 the choir was prolonged by about 4 mt. thereby including in the building the tower of a noble family; the transept was enlarged as well, with three chapels on each side after a plan by the Florentine Giuliano da Majano to whom was also commissioned the plan of the chapel of St. Fina in 1468 through which we come to the right aisle: symmetrically opposite to it is the chapel of the Conception built in 1477. The wooden pulpit is attributed to Antonio da Colle (ca.

5

1469), probably also the author of the pews by the left wall. Rear-façade wall - Below, the remains of a small apse belonging to the original oratory with floor at a lower level than the present church's. On the side of the left aisle are remains of a 13th-cent. *St. Christopher* and fragments of frescoes, one of which represents the *Consecration of the Parish* while other are of uncertain meaning and, on the lunette of the door, *Madonna with Child between two Saints* framed by a triangular pediment with two worshipping Angels: a sum payed in 1305 to Memmo di Filippuccio, Sienese painter and father of the better known Lippo, whose artistic personality has been recently evaluated by critics, is undoubtedly related to these works. Near the nave and above the first two arches dividing it from the aisles, a grandiose representation of the *Last Judgement* is displayed with *Judging Christ* in the middle, the Virgin and the Baptist, Prophets Enoch and Elijah, Angels and the 12 Apostles: to the right is *Heaven* (the gap in the middle was caused by a bombing in 1944) and, to the left, *Hell* harshly expressive and bearing on the lower part the name of Taddeo di Bartolo da Siena who painted the frescoes in 1408 or 1413. Below the main episode is a big scene enclosed by a rich framing representing the *Martyrdom of St. Sebastian* signed by Benozzo Fiorentino (better known as Gozzoli) and dated 1465, and below it a panel with a *Crucifix adored by St. Jerome and St. Paul Hermit*. Also by Gozzoli and his

collaborators are, on both sides of the painting, *Our Lady of the Assumption* and *St. Anthony Abbot*: the images of *St. Fina* and *St. Catherine of Alexandria with two devout women on their knees* on the external sides of the pilasters are gentle creations attrib. to Lippo Memmi (ca. 1318). On the corners between wall and pilasters are two remarkable wooden statues of the *Annunciating Angel* and the *Annunciated Virgin* sculptured in 1421 by Jacopo della Quercia (who signed the Angel on the base) and painted in 1426 by Martino di Bartolomeo.

Right aisle - The whole wall is occupied by a cycle of frescoes representing the *Stories of the New Testament* arranged on three orders, with the *Crucifixion* taking the space of four Stories. The narration begins with *Annunciation* in the right lunette and goes on for five more lunettes until the *Flight into Egypt*; then it comes back towards the façade from *Jesus among the Doctors* to *Entrance to Jerusalem* and, in the lower order, it continues again from right to left from *Last Supper* to *Crucifixion*, beyond which were four more stories about events occurred after Christ's death, mostly destroyed when a chancel was added in the 16th cent. now destroyed as well. According to Vasari's opinion these frescoes have long been considered to be by the Sienese Barna (or Berna), who died allegedly falling from a scaffolding while working at them, so that they were finished by his follower Giovanni d'Asciano. Recent art critics, however, have even denied the

existence of Barna (although he was mentioned as a painter in a Sienese document of 1340) and ascribe them to Lippo Memmi, thus giving credit to a graffito inscription discovered in 1927 on one of the episodes: «Lipo da Siena pinxit», and to the name «Lipo» found on other parts. It should also be noted that so roughly engraved an inscription can hardly be defined a signature and also that Vasari never wrote one of his «Lives» about an artist who was not or did not later turn out to be documented. However, the works which were with certainty painted by Lippo Memmi, although sharing the same culture, focused on Simone Martini, of the frescoes concerned (which show themes typical of Giotto and Duccio's iconographical schemes, unusual in Memmi's works), are characterized by a refined elegance of lines and by an intimate and aristocratic language which is far from the sober and sharp profiles and from the robust plasticism of these Episodes. These, in fact, are imbued with an unrestrained, almost popular expressiveness often reaching a dramatic tension hardly equalled in Sienese painting. It is therefore probable that the originally creative person active in the 4th or 5th decade of the 14th cent., and possibly helped by collaborators like Giovanni d'Asciano, is to be identified with

Barna himself, whose tragic death was reported on an epigraph (destroyed long ago) which must have been the expression of an old and reliable local tradition. Among the most intense and dramatic scenes of the whole cycle, apart from the grandiose *Crucifixion*, the following are of particular interest: *Judas' pact*, *Christ's capture*, the *Scourging* and *Ascent to Calvary*. Six *Prophets* by collaborators and followers of Barna are represented on the opposite arches while *St. Gregory appearing to St. Fina* to predict her coming death and the celestial award on the seventh lunette has been attributed to Niccolò di Segna.

At the end of the aisle, on the right, is the *chapel of St. Fina*, Patron saint of S. Gimignano, built in very elegant forms of the purest Florentine Renaissance in 1468 by Giuliano da Majano: the altar, inside an arch, with a beautiful marble pavilion, is by Giuliano's brother, Benedetto da Majano, who finished it in 1475. On the altar frontal is the Saint's sarcophagus overlooked by a *Virgin with Child* inside a mandorla of seraphs adored by two Angels: the altar table with underlying pilasters is by Tito Sarrocchi (1881). The wall frescoes are among the most genuine and poetic creations by the Florentine Domenico Bigordi called «Ghirlandaio» who painted them befo-

re 1475. To the right is the *Apparition of St. Gregory to St. Fina* who is seen lying on a rough table; under it are the gillyflowers into which the mice eating the crumbs of her bread were turned and, to the left, is the *Funeral of the Saint*, a scene of clear outline with St. Fina surrounded by the clergy and the citizens of S. Gimignano: the nurse Beldia, with a paralyzed hand, and a blind altar-boy are healed by touching the Saint's body while bells are rung by Angels. The Four *Evangelists* on the vault, the *Doctors of the Church* and the *Prophets* on the arch pendentives are also attributed to Ghirlandaio.

Transept - The walls are decorated above by Giovanni Cambi from S. Gimignano (1503) except the *Baptist* in the first tondo to the left, painted by a follower of Barna. On the altar of the right end, *Supper in Emmaus* by Gaetano Cannicci from S. Gimignano (1848), the father of the better known painter Niccolò. The choir, flanked by couples of richly decorated chapels, has two orders of seats dated 1490 and attrib. to Antonio da Colle: on the high altar, under a big wooden *Crucifix* by Antonio Noferi (1754) is a beautiful marble ciborium with two Angels at its sides by Benedetto da Majano (1475) and, at the left end is a canvas with the *Invention of the Cross* attrib. to the Florentine Niccolò Lapi, pupil and collaborator of Luca Giordano.

Left aisle - *Chapel of Conception* of 1477, restored in the 17th cent.; over the altar a panel painting with *Immaculate Conception* attrib. to Ludovico Cardi called «Cigoli» and, on the walls, a *Virgin's Nativity* and *St. Filippo Neri and St. Francesco of Sales before an altar with Annunciated Virgin* by the Florentine Pier Dandini (1701). Under the organ chancel (1467) is the entrance door to the Baptistery built inside a Romanesque loggia beside the Parish walls: on the end wall a beautiful fresco of the *Annunciation* (to which the chapel was previously dedicated), formerly attrib. to Ghirlandaio although it is one of the gentle creations by Sebastiano Mainardi, dated 1482. Below the painting is a marble creation of 1379 by Giovanni di Cecco from Siena, the only signed work of this sculptor who was master builder in the Sienese Duomo for a long time. On a vaulting cell is a noble figure of *Prophet* attrib. to Barna. We come back into the

The Cathedral or Collegiate Church of S. Maria Assunta: 1. The entry into Jerusalem, fresco by Barna; 2. Chapel of S. Fina: over the altar frontal is the sarcophagus of the Saint; 3. St. Gregorio foretelling St. Fina the coming death, fresco by Ghirlandaio; 4. The killing of Job's servants, by Bartolo di Fredi.

2

3

church where *Stories of the Old Testament* are displayed on the whole wall, frescoed in 1367 by Bartolo di Fredi who signed and dated them. The cycle runs on three orders, all of them arranged from left to right, starting from the façade, and is characterized by a narrative and colouring liveliness. Among the most remarkable scenes are *Job's banquet*, *Earthquake in Job's house*, and above all the *Passing of the Red Sea and the drowning of the Pharaoh's army*, rich in interesting details about the clothing and the habits of those times.

On the lunettes above the opposite arches are *Abraham* attrib. to Gozzoli and six *Prophets* by Pier Francesco Fiorentino (1474). Beside the parish is a beautiful cloister, formerly a cemetery, from the second half of the 16th century, which can be reached through Piazza Pecori. Here, in an old dormitory for chaplains, the MUSEO D'ARTE SACRA (Museum of Sacred Art) was set up in 1930, and contains works coming from the Collegiate and from other Sienese churches.

On the right side of the Collegiate is the Piazza delle Erbe beyond which, through Via della Rocca, we go up to the ROCCA (stronghold), with a pentagon-shaped plan, erected in 1353 and demolished in 1558 by Cosimo I; from its remains and out of one of its large keeps a suggestive views of the town towers is offered.

Leaving Piazza della Collegiata and passing under the double ARCO DELLA CANCELLERIA, an old gate in the earliest town walls, we enter Via S. Matteo, the main street of the town, which, for the

4

1

medieval look of its houses and palaces, most of them preserved in their original appearance, is now an area of rare beauty. Beyond the PALAZZO DELLA CANCEL-LERIA, to the right is the Romanesque CHURCH OF S. BARTOLO with a façade of Pisan-style bricks, and then the imposing PESCIOLINI TOWER-HOUSE of the late 13th cent., in Florentine style, having on its upper floors two orders of two-light mullioned windows; further ahead is TINAC-CI PALACE, formed by two buildings, admirably merging architectural elements of Florence, Lucca and Siena. Before reaching PORTA S. MATTEO from 1262, at the end of the street, we turn right into Via Cellolese and reach Piazza S. Agostino on the right side of which is the Romanesque CHURCH OF S. PIETRO; in the interior, frescoes by Memmo di Filippuccio and one of his collaborators, probably the young Barna: *Virgin with Child between St. Catherine and Magdalene - Annunciation - Adoration of the Magi* and others. The **CHURCH OF S. AGOSTINO**, consecrated in 1298, has a bare outside made of bricks with sides crowned by small arches. The interior has a single wide nave ending with a rectangular choir flanked by two chapels. At the wall of the rear-façade is the chapel of S. Bartolo (Bartolo, of the noble family of the Buonpedoni, after spending his youth and maturity in assisting the sick and the poor, caught leprosy which made him blind; after enduring the illness with exemplary submission, which procured him the title of «Job of Tuscany», he died in 1300 at the age of 72). The altar-tomb is one of the last and most beautiful creations by Benedetto da Majano, finished in 1495 and made of an altar frontal with three Theological Virtues overlooked by a garland with the Virgin and Child adored by two Angels. Under the sarcophagus is a predella with 3 stories depicting the miracle of a Saint's toe being reattached after it had remained in the hands of a priest washing his feet, the Saint's death and the healing of a possessed woman. The four *Doctors of the Church* on the vault and the *St. Gimignano, Lucia and Nicola of Bari* on the wall were frescoed by Sebastiano Mainardi (1500). Then, in the nave, an altar-piece with the *Virgin and Child with 7 Saints*, with predella, signed and dated 1494 by Pier Francesco Fiorentino. Beyond the lateral door, *Christ's pietà between the Virgin and St. John and the*

2

Passion instruments, votive fresco by Bartolo di Fredi, then a *Crucifixion* by the same author, an altar with a statue of *St. Nicola of Tolentino* of the 16th cent., frescoes attrib. to Vincenzo Tamagni (1529) and a canvas with *Mystical wedding of St. Catherine of Siena* attrib. to a follower of Ventura Salimbeni. A chapel to the right of the choir is frescoed with *Stories of the Virgin* by Bartolo di Fredi (ca. 1374) and it has a *Virgin's nativity* on the altar, signed by Vincenzo Tamagni (1523). On the high altar is a grandiose panel painting with *Crowning of the Virgin adored by 6 Saints* signed and dated 1483 by Piero del Pollaiolo, younger brother of better known Antonio. The choir walls are frescoed with a cycle of *Stories of St. Augustine* painted in 1464-65 by Benozzo Gozzoli, admirable for the richness and effectiveness of its episodes, for its noble and clear architectural perspectives and for its pleasant background landscapes. The tale starts from the lowest order and must be read from left to right even in the middle order and in the lunettes: 1 - *Augustine accompanied to Tagaste by his parents to his grammar teacher*; 2 - *He is received into Carthage's University*; 3 - *He is blessed at a distance by his mother Monica* (repainted in the 18th cent.); 4 - *He travels to Italy by sea*; 5 - *He is received to Italy by an important person*; 6 - *He lectures Rethoric and Philosophy in Rome*; 7 - *He leaves for Milan*; 8 - *He is received in Milan by St. Ambrogio*; 9 - *He speaks with St. Ambrogio and listens to one of his omilies*; 10 - *He reads St. Paul's epistles and is converted by them*; 11 - *He is baptized by St. Ambrogio*; 12 - *He visits the hermits of Mount Pisano*; 13 - *St. Monica's death*; 14 - *After being consecrated bishop he blesses the people of Ippona*;

3

15 - *He converts heretic Fortunato*; 16 - *He writes inspired by God*; 17 - *Saint's funeral*. On the vault *Four Evangelists*, on the underside of the entrance arch *Christ and the Apostles* and, on the pilasters, *12 Saints* and two stories, also by Gozzoli and his collaborators. In the left chapel *Mystical wedding of St. Catherine of Alexandria and 8 Saints*, panel painting signed and dated 1589 by the Florentine Giovanni Balducci called «Cosci» and *Virgin with Child and Saints* by brother Paolino da Pistoia (1530). Going down into the nave, *St. Gimignano blessing three famous inhabitants of the town* (poet Mattia Lupi, canonist Domenico Mainardi and jurist Nello de' Cetti) by Sebastiano Mainardi (1487) and a slab with busts of bishops attrib. to Tino da Camaino. Then is the altar of the *Virgin of the Graces* with fresco (partly repainted) by Lippo Memmi and, beyond the pulpit (1524), *St. Sebastian Interceding*, a fresco of great iconographical interest by Benozzo Gozzoli (1464) and *Adoration of the Cross*, fresco attrib. to Vincenzo Tamagni. Beside the church is a beautiful cloister of the late 15th cent.

Leaving Piazza S. Agostino and going through Via Marconi we reach Via Folgore da S. Gimignano where, to the right, are the *Spedale of St. Fina* (1203) hav-

ing in its vestibule the busts of *St. Fina* and *St. Gregory* by Pietro Torrigiano and frescoes by Mainardi, the *Church of S. Domenico* (on its altar is a *St. Jerome and the lion*, fresco attrib. to Mainardi) and, at the end, the small Romanesque church of *S. Jacopo dei Templari* (inside are a *Crucifixion* and a *Virgin with Jesus between St. James and St. John Evangelist* attrib. to Memmo di Filippuccio).

Through the nearby PORTA S. JACOPO we go down to PORTA ALLE FONTI and then to the *Fonti* (fountains) with 10 arches of the 13th and 14th cent.: coming up Via delle Fonti and Via delle Romite, beyond the ARCO DI S. STEFANO IN CANOVA we reach the former CONVENT OF S. DOMENICO (now a prison), built on the area where the old castle of the bishop stood. On Via del Castello is the CHURCH OF S. LORENZO IN PONTE of 1240 which contains frescoes by the Florentine Cenni di Francesco di Ser Cenni (1413): the old *Spezieria* (Drug collection) of the Spedale of S. Fina, consisting of a rich series of ceramic chemist's pots with various forms from the 15th to the 18th cent., is temporarily set up in the church. Via del Castello, with beautiful medieval houses, ends into Piazza della Cisterna.

Church of S. Agostino: 1. Martyrdom of St. Sebastian, by Benozzo Gozzoli; 2. The interior; 3. Crowning of the Virgin, by Piero del Pollaiolo.

S. QUIRICO D'ORCIA

Continuing onto the Via Cassia, after passing through *Torrenieri*, at km. 44.2 we go up to **S. Quirico D'Orcia**, an old village which was once the seat of an imperial vicariate. In front of us, just inside the entrance, we see the PARISH CHURCH OF S. QUIRICO IN OSENNA of the 12th cent., rebuilt at the end of the 13th cent. Its façade has a grandiose and richly ornamented Romanesque portal and, on one side, a portal of the late 13th cent. with two imposing caryatids resting on lions by a probably Umbrian follower of Giovanni Pisano and another portal dated 1298. The interior, with a Latin cross shape, contains a wonderful altar piece by Sano di Pietro and, in the choir, seats with backs admirably figured with inlaids by Antonio Barili (1428-1505) coming from the chapel of S. Giovanni del Duomo in Siena: then a canvas with the *Virgin of the Rosary saving a drowned girl* attrib. to Rutilio Manetti. Behind the parish is the austere CHIGI PALACE by Carlo Fontana (late 17th cent.). The street running through the whole village is Via Dante Alighieri (on its right stands the 15th-cent. PRETORIO PALACE, flanked by medieval houses) and it reaches Piazza della Libertà where, on the left, is the CHURCH OF S. MARIA DI VITALETA (which contains a *Madonna* by Della Robbia and two wooden statues of *Annunciation* from the 1st half of the 15th cent., attrib. to an artist close to Francesco di Valdambrino), and, on the right, the entrance to the ORTI LEONINI, the most beautiful park in the province of Siena, set up by Diomede Leoni (ca.1540). Going ahead, towards the end of the road is the Romanesque *small Church of S. Maria* with a portal built using materials from the Abbey of S. Antimo.

MONTALCINO

Leaving the Via Cassia, about 2 km. past Buonconvento (see 2nd tour), a road of about 8 km. to the right goes up to **Montalcino** (564 mt. above sea-level), a small town lying on a hill in a very pleasant landscape, rich of olive-trees and vineyards, sloping down to the valleys of the rivers Orcia, Ombrone and Asso. The town, whose origins date back to very remote times and formerly a feud of S. Antimo Abbey, was contended between Siena and Florence, until the Sienese brought it under their domination in 1260. Montalcino is also renowned for the strenuous resistance opposed to the imperial army of don Garcia Toledo by the Sienese exiles who left their town after its fall in 1555. Their leader Pietro Strozzi gave Montalcino institutions similar to those of the conquered Republic and had coins minted with the motto «Libertas et Resp. Sen. in Monte Ilcino»: according to the peace of Câteau-Cambrésis, however, the French garrison troops were moved away and Montalcino was submitted to the Medici in 1559.

On arriving, we see, on top of the hill, an imposing STRONGHOLD built by the Sienese in 1361 over part of the 13th-cent. walls to which the keep of S. Martino and the large tower of S. Giovanni belong. Through a gate bearing the emblem of Siena we enter a wide courtyard with the remains of an ancient small church: from its interior, where a Sienese banner by the school of Sodoma and other mementoes are preserved, we reach the watch walk-way from which a a view of the beautiful landscape is offered. Piazza del Popolo is the centre of Montalcino onto which looks a *Loggia* from the 14th-15th cent. and, on one corner, is the TOWN HALL of 1285, finished in the 14th cent. and flanked by a slender tower of stone and bricks (whose upper part is from the 16th cent.). On the side of the palace looking onto the square is a wide arcade on the ground floor with a statue of *Cosimo I* by Giovanni Berti (1564). We walk along the Town Hall up to a small square where the CHURCH OF S. EGIDIO stands, called «dei Senesi» because the Sienese built it over an older one in 1325. Going upwards, to the right, is the Gothic CHURCH OF S. AGOSTINO of the 14th cent., with a beautiful rose-window on its façade and containing fragments of frescoes attrib. to Bartolo di Fredi. On one side is a former Seminary with two 16th-cent. cloisters: in the former chapter hall is a big *Crucifixion* frescoed in monochrome on a red background probably by Carlo di Giovanni (mid-15th cent.). In this room and in adjoining ones are the UNITED MUNICIPAL AND DIOCESAN MUSEUMS.

Spagni we go up to the **Cathedral**, built in Neoclassical style over the ancient parish of S. Salvatore, by Agostino Fantastici (1818-34); its interior contains an *Immaculate Conception* signed and dated 1588 by Francesco Vanni. Then we walk down to the CHURCH OF MADONNA DEL SOCCORSO with a modern façade and a Baroque interior, from which, turning right into Viale Roma, we reach Piazza Cavour onto which looks a long building from the 16th cent., the seat of the Library; one of its rooms, formerly the pil-

3

4

5

grim's room, later turned into the pharmacy of the old Spedale of S. Maria della Croce, has walls frescoed in 1510-12 by Vincenzo Tamagni. Immediately outside the town is the Gothic CHURCH OF S. FRANCESCO, restored in the 16th and 18th cent., whose interior and adjoining hospital contains more frescoes, although damaged, by Tamagni.

Leaving the Stronghold on a road winding among the vineyards which produce «Brunello», one of the most valuable Italian wines, we reach a secluded valley, at about 6 km., where the famous ABBEY OF S. ANTIMO rises, whose church is «the most important Romanesque monument in Southern Tuscany». The Benedictine community who lived at the Abbey, founded in Carolingian times, owned a very large territory and, from the 10th to 12th cent., its Abbots had the title of Counts of the Holy Roman Empire and a temporal power over Montalcino. In 1291 the Benedictine monks were replaced by the Guglielmiti and in 1462 the Abbey was suppressed and joined to the diocese of Montalcino by Pius II. The present church was built in the 1st half of the 12th cen. by Benedictine monks according to a Lombard Romanesque style strongly influenced by French features. Its longitudinal plan with a nave and two aisles, the latter being prolonged to the apsidal area forming a peribolos from which three sunburst arranged chapels start, is in fact typical of a representational system rarely used in Italy and very popular in Burgundy. Cruciform piers among the columns and the women's galleries are also northern themes. The outside, made of travertine, has two portals on the sides, with 9th-cent. decorations and a powerful square bell tower in Lombard style rises at the end of the building, while the beautiful back of the church is visible behind it, with the

three chapels protruding from the apse. Its simple façade shows the remains of four blind arches and a prothyrum before a rich portal, on the architrave of which is the name of an architect monk called Azzone de' Porcari. The interior has a very slender nave and the right aisle is larger than the left one; the sense of depth is enhanced by the narrowing of both nave and aisles towards the apse. Some architectural elements are made of a special onyx coming from the nearby quarry of Castelnuovo, with alabaster-like brightness and transparence. Particular mention should be made of the figured capitals, all different from one another, some of which (like the 2nd to the right, with *Daniel in the lions' den*) are attrib. to «Maestro di Cabestany», the greatest Catalan sculptor of the 12th century. On the altar predella is an inscription of 1117 while a beautiful polychrome wood *Enthroned Madonna* of 13th-cent. Umbrian-Sienese school is now in the Art Gallery of Siena and will be placed in its original position over the altar, inside a temperature-controlled case. Beside the entrance are parts of Romanesque sculptures formerly belonging to the prothyrum. There is also a big wooden *Crucifix* of the late 12th cent. Through a stair on the right of the altar we enter a small crypt with an altar table which was once a Roman tomb slab (347 A.D.) and under the bell tower is a small three-apse chapel. From the sacristy, with walls frescoed in black and white during the 15th cent., we go up to the

S. Quirico d'Orcia: 1. Collegiate church; 2. Orti Leonini. Montalcino: 3. Town Hall of 1285; 4. The stronghold of 1361; 5. The romanesque abbey of S. Antimo.

women's gallery on the right aisle, turned into an apartment for the Abbot, formed by 5 rooms, in the 15th cent., and under the sacristy (entrance from outside) there is a hall with a nave and two aisles (probably a crypt or a Carolingian church), divided by 4 columns. Some remains of the monastery are on a square at the right of the church, once probably a cloister.

On a hill south of the Abbey, at about 3 km., is the small village of CASTELNUOVO DELL'ABATE from which a road of ca. 4 km. leads down to the *Station of Mount Amiata*.

MOUNT AMIATA

The Mount, called in ancient times *Mons Tusciae* and later *Mons ad Meata*, is an imposing trachyte rock of volcanic origin rising up to 1734 mt. above sea-level among the valleys of the rivers Orcia, Fiore and Ombrone, and is the highest peak in Tuscany south of the Arno, rich in chestnut and beech woods, where many springs provide with water Siena, the Maremma and the area around Viterbo. The Mount Amiata, for its natural beauty, the charm of its ancient tradition and the picturesque villages dotting its slopes, represents an ideal place for excursions, summer holidays and winter sports. An excursion to the Mount Amiata starts from the Station where a carriage road, past a bridge over the Orcia, leads after 11 km. to **SEGGIANO**. Just outside the village is the ORATORY OF S. ROCCO of 1496 with frescoes by Girolamo di Domenico (1490-93). In the town hall is a polyptych by the Sienese «Maestro di Panzano» (ca. 1370) and in the parish church, is a dismembered *polyptych* by «Maestro d'Ovile». Along the road, on the right, is the *Sanctuary of the Madonna della Carità*, a peculiar votive building of the late 16th cent. with a high dome covered with fired bricks. About 11 km. ahead we enter **CASTELDELPIANO** (634 mt. above sea-level, in the province of Grosseto), an important holiday resort whose main street is flanked by 16th-century buildings which give it a townlike appearance: the street is named after the *Nasini*, a family of painters of the 17th and 18th cent., very active in the region of the Amiata, in Siena, Florence and Rome. In the middle of Casteldelpiano, on Piazza della Madonna, is the *Prepositura*, called «*Church of the Opera*», with a refinedly decorated façade of trachyte from the 17th cent., finished in 1870. Its interior, with 10 chapels, contains a number of paintings by the Nasini and their followers, a *Beheading of the Baptist* attrib. to Alessandro Casolani, a

Miracle of St. Cerbone by D. Manetti and a scenographic high altar attrib. to the Mazzuoli brothers (18th cent). To the left is the CHURCH OF GRAZIE, with a rich 19th-century façade inspired by Renaissance features: in the interior, the revered image of the *Madonna delle Grazie* is an imitation from Sano di Pietro. On the right of Corso Nasini is an ancient district with the graceful Piazzetta degli Ortaggi having a characteristic small loggia under a 16th-century palace.

Beyond Casteldelpiano, to the right, is a CAPUCHIN CONVENT in whose church is a beautiful canvas signed and dated 1593 by Francesco Vanni (*Virgin on throne adored by the St. Bernardino, Francis and Leonard*), and, 3 km. further, we reach **ARCIDOSSO** (661 mt. above sea-level, in the province of Grosseto). This old village, with long and winding streets flanked by houses made of trachyte blocks, is overlooked by the huge mass of the medieval ROCCA ALDOBRANDESCA. Arcidosso is known for being the native place (1834) of David Lazzaretti, called «Saint David» and «the Amiata prophet», founder of the sect of the «Giurisdavidici» who, by preaching a religious and civil reformation with attention to social problems, originated a wide-spread phenomenon of collective mysticism hardly equalled in 19th-century Italy. Lazzaretti was killed in 1878 by the police. We enter the town's centre through the scenographic PORTA DELL'OROLOGIO (19th cent.) and, past the CHURCH OF S. NICCOLÒ, with a façade in false Romanesque style (1934), we reach the CHURCH OF S. LEONARDO, founded in the Middle Ages although enlarged in the late 17th century. Its interior contains

4 panel paintings of the late 16th cent. by unknown artists, a *Beheading of the Baptist* by Francesco Vanni (1589) and two remarkable wooden statues of *St. Processo* and *St. Andrea* dated 1617. At the south-west border of the village stands the SANCTUARY OF THE MADONNA DELLE GRAZIE, a beautiful construction built after the 1348 plague, though of late 15th-century character, inspired by Peruzzi's style, with a dome from the 2nd half of the 16th century. Over its high altar of 1689 is a panel painting with *Virgin with Child* by Pellegrino di Mariano (15th cent.) and, in the right chapel, is a two-sided altar-piece by Ventura Salimbeni (*Virgin of the Snow* and *Virgin in Glory with St. Sebastian and Roch*).

Past BAGNORE, a village with springs of sulphureous water, we reach, 8 km. farther on, **SANTA FIORA** (687 mt. above sea-level, in the province of Grosseto), formerly belonging to the Abbey of S. Salvatore, later a fief of the Aldobrandeschi (11th-15th cent.) then, from 1439 onwards, of the Sforza of Cotignola, and finally of the Sforza Cesarini. From Piazza Garibaldi in the centre, onto which the façade of the SFORZA CESARINI PALACE looks, together with the MUNICIPAL TOWER of the 15th cent., we go down along the picturesque, old village to the Romanesque-Gothic PARISH OF SS. FLORA AND LUCILLA, which still contains an important series of glazed terra-cottas: altar-piece with *Assumption of the Virgin* by Andrea della Robbia (ca.1490), triptych with *Crowning of the Virgin*, altar-piece with *Christ's baptism*

Mount Amiata: 1. Winter sports facilities on the mount; 2. The monumental iron Cross.

and *pulpit* by the workshop of Andrea della Robbia. Further downwards is the *Church of S. Agostino* (in the interior are wooden statues among which a beautiful *Madonna* by the school of Jacopo della Quercia) and then the PESCHIERA, a wide, enclosed basin from the 18th cent. which receives water from the springs which form the Flora river. If we do not take the road to Castellazzara, where, at about 6 km., is the CONVENT OF SELVA with a big altare-piece representing the *Assumption* by Girolamo di Benvenuto (ca. 1500), the trip to Mount Amiata continues for 12 km. to **PIAN-CASTAGNAIO** (772 above sea-level), which overlooks the Valle della Paglia, formerly belonging to the Abbey of S. Salvatore, contended among the Aldobrandeschi and finally come under the Sienese domination in 1415. On the highest point in the village rises the powerful 14th-cent. ROCCA ALDOBRANDESCA with a square plan, a keep and a large tower, and, at the opposite end, BOURBON DEL MONTE PALACE of 1603-11 in a late 16th-cent. style: in the picturesque district at mid-level, is the PARISH OF ASSUNTA, probably of the 13th cent., although restored, which can be reached through a stairway. More interesting are the churches lying just outside the centre: the *Church of S. Maria delle Grazie* with frescoes attrib. to Nanni di Pietro, probably from Orvieto (mid-15th cent.), the SANCTUARY OF MADONNA DI S. PIETRO with a rich series of frescoes by Francesco Nasini (1640) who represented here, the «*Novissimi*» (the four things man is confronted with at his life's end) and the CHURCH OF THE CONVENT OF S. FRANCESCO containing, in the choir, fragments of a dramatic *Slaughter of the Innocents* of Sienese school of the mid-14th century.

About 5 km. from Piancastagnaio lies **ABBADIA S. SALVATORE** (700 mt. above sea-level), named after a famous ABBEY which, although not the oldest, was the richest in Tuscany. According to tradition it was founded in 743 by the Langobard king Ratchis, and it received a number of privileges and concessions by Charlemagne, Ludovic the Pius and their successors. It was the seat first of the Black Benedictine, then of the Cistercian, from 1230 to the suppression of Leopoldo II in 1783: the Cistercian have been reinstated here since 1939. The adjoining small village was established as a free City-State with its own Statutes in 1210 and in 1347 it was annexed to the Sienese State. Not much is left of the old wealth of the Abbey which had a rich library, with the famous «Amiata Bible», an Irish work of the 7th cent., presently in the Laurenziana Library in Florence.

The church, consecrated in 1036, has a sloping façade flanked by two towers (one of which is unfinished), which makes it one of the rare Italian examples of nordic «Westerwerk». The interior has a single wide nave with truss roof and big arches over a raised presbyterium which can be reached through a stairway. To the right is a big wooden *Crucifix* of the late 12th cent., the oldest wooden sculpture in the Sienese territory, and, in front of it, a *Martyrdom of S. Bartholomew*, a fresco by Francesco Nasini dated 1694. More frescoes by the same author are in the presbyterium area and in the chapels, particularly the chapel at the right of the choir, where *Stories of Ratchis* narrating the abbey's foundation are represented. The underlying crypt, with a cross-shaped plan and 35 columns with shafts and capitals different from one another, is usually wrongly considered the primitive Langobard church: it dates instead from the 11th cent. and Abbot Winizzone was buried there in 1036. In an adjoining monastery an Irish *reliquary* of the 7th cent. and a *Reliquary-Bust of Pope St. Mark* of gilded copper and enamels dated 1381 are preserved.

In more recent times tourist and industrial activities have been given a significant boost, both because it is the only winter sport resort in the province of Siena, and because it lies at 1 km. from a mercury mine which is the most productive in Europe ranking second only after Spain, with also a plant for cinnabar mining. It is also a starting point for excursions to the peak of the Mount Amiata (1739 mt.) called «Sasso di Maremma», on which a huge, 22 mt.-high cross of wrought-iron rises. It was built by the Sienese workshop of Luciano Zalaffi in 1910, destroyed during the last war and rebuilt in 1946; a view of the beautiful landscape is offered from the cross, ranging from the Tyrrhenian Sea with the Island of Elba and Corsica to the Cimini Mountains, the Terminillo, the Gran Sasso and the peaks of the Tuscan-Emilian Apennines. At 1651 mt., in a place which can be reached on a 12.5 km.-long carriage road, are hotels, restaurants and skilifts.

From Abbadia S. Salvatore we can either go down directly to the Via Cassia, which we join in «Le Conie», or continue to CAMPIGLIA D'ORCIA at 12 km.; then we take a road to the left which goes up to **Vivo d'Orcia** (3.2 km.) in a beautiful position among woods and meadowlands. Near the village is the HERMI-

TAGE OF S. BENEDETTO, allegedly founded by St. Romualdo, formerly belonging to the Camaldolesian and destroyed in 1387. Later it was a property of the Farnese and, in 1534, of the Cervini of Montepulciano, who built there a fortified palace attrib. to Antonio da Sangallo the Jounger. It was the favourite residence of future Pope Marcellus II. Another 10 km. ahead we reach **CASTIGLIONE D'ORCIA**, a picturesque village near the remains of the Aldobrandeschi Castle of S. Fiora, later a property of the Salimbeni of Siena. It is the native place of the painter and sculptor Lorenzo di Pietro called «Vecchietta», after whom the suggestive small square is named, with a well of 1618 and, on one side, the Town Hall. In the PARISH OF SS. STEFANO AND DEGNA, with a 15th-cent. façade and 16th-cent. frescoes, the left chapel, closed by a screen, contains three beautiful panel paintings representing the *Virgin with Child*: two of them are by Pietro Lorenzetti and Vecchietta, while the third is attrib. to Simone Martini. At a short distance is **Rocca d'Orcia**, overlooked by a huge, polygonal *Stronghold* called «of Tentennano», previously belonging to the Salimbeni. In the upper part of the village, partly retaining its medieval character, is the CHURCH OF S. SIMEONE containing a beautiful panel painting of the *Nursing Virgin* by Giovanni di Paolo. The Amiata excursion is completed by returning to the Via Cassia, about 4 km. from Rocca d'Orcia, at about 45 km. from Siena.

SAN GALGANO

Again on the Road 73, beyond the bridge over the Feccia, we turn left in direction Monticiano and then right into the Strada Massetana, and we see the ABBEY OF S. GALGANO (33 km. from Siena), whose massive remains rise in the valley of the Merse. A noble, 32 years old knight, Galgano Guidotti da Chiusdino, retired there in 1180 to lead a life of penance; a big monastery was built starting from the early 13th cent. and became then the centre of the Tuscan Cistercian. Works were carried out by monks, probably the same monks who had worked at the Badia of Casamari in the region of Lazio, and lasted from 1224, when the Abbey reached an advanced constructive state, to 1288, when cloister and capitular hall were finished. Legacies, donations, papal and imperial privileges soon enriched the Community, thus giving it a wide prestige; its monks were therefore often questioned about issues related to the Sienese Commune and they

were entrusted with the administration of the Opera del Duomo from 1258 to 1285.

During the 15th cent. the monastery began to decline and in 1503 it became a commendam: as a consequence of the unconcern of commendatory Abbots, the building was soon ruined. In 1632 it lost its privilege as an Abbey and was secularized: large cracks opened in its walls and, in the 18th cent., vaults and bell tower collapsed, turning this previously flourishing cultural centre into a desolate state.

The church is in Cistercian-Gothic style, mostly of French character, although with some local elements, and its importance lies in its being the oldest prove of the penetration of transalpine architecture into Tuscany. Its unfinished, simple façade, before which an arcade should have been built, has three round-arched doors with ogival extradosses and the lateral walls are interrupted above by buttresses alternating with two-light, and, below, with one-light windows. The interior, with a nave and two aisles and 69 mt. long, is extremely suggestive with its wide nave flooded by light; the grass on the floor is limited by two rows of cruciform pilasters connected to one another by ogival arches with double lintels. At

3 mt. of height are columns, resting on the said arches, which rise until the wall top where they support big ogival arches from which vaults once started. The transept has a nave and two aisles, the eastern one being divided into four chapels which flank the rectangular choir: this is lit up by two orders of one-light windows and by a big, circular oculus and a smaller oculus above. On the right of the church rose once the cloister, of which only a short part is left. Particularly interesting in the monastery — presently inhabited by a community of Olivetan nuns — are the capitular hall, with two aisles divided by squat columns, and the refectory, also two-aisled, divided by pilasters and with a vaulted ceiling.

On the hill of Montesiepi, above, rises the small CHURCH OF S. GALGANO built near a rock into which knight Galgano, according to a legend, drove his sword to adore its cross-shaped hilt (although the present sword is modern). It is a peculiar building, with a circular plan, whose outside is partly covered by white and black bands, also repeated in concentric circles in the dome's interior.

S. Galgano: 1. 2. Cistercian abbey; 3. Romanesque small church of S. Galgano; Monte Oliveto Maggiore: 4. The Abbey's apse and belltower; 5. One wing of the Big Cloister with the cycle of frescoes devoted to St. Benedict. 6. The Big Cloister, fresco by Luca Signorelli (cycle of stories of St. Benedict); 7. The choir reading-desk, by brother Raffaele da Brescia; 8. The refectory; 9. The Big Cloister.

of the late 14th cent.: on the outside is a *Virgin with Child* and, inside, *St. Benedict*, 16th-cent. statues of glazed terra-cotta, carried out with a technique typical of Della Robbia, although not under his influence. The wood is dotted with chapels, the oldest of which is that of *St. Scolastica*, with a Romanesque apse having a bowl-shaped vault frescoed by brother Antonio da Bologna (1516) while the richest of them is the one built in 1760 on the cave in which Blessed Bernardo lived as an hermit, with an elegant façade after a plan attrib. to Francesco Galli Bibiena. A road paved with bricks, passing by a fish-weir of 1533 by G.B. Pelori, goes down to the abbey flanked by a church (1401-17) with its 18th-cent. polygonal apse and a late-Gothic bell tower finished in 1466. After entering the monastery, beyond a vestibule and a passage hall, we come to a 15th-century «big cloister», with a well from 1439 and walls frescoed with *Stories of St. Benedict* which form the widest iconographic cycle devoted to the Saint, inspired by St. Benedict's life as drawn from the 2nd Book of the «Dialogues» by St. Gregorius Magnus. Nine Stories in the west wing were painted by Luca Signorelli (1497-99), while the remaining stories were carried out from 1505 to 1508 by Giov. Antonio Bazzi called «Sodoma» from Vercelli, except the first one in the west wing which is by Riccio (1536). The narration, however, begins in the east wing and an Italian inscription under each story explains the meaning of the scene. The nine episodes frescoed by Signorelli are admirable for their strong plasticity and the monumentality of figures and groups sharply arranged inside airy perspective

MONTEOLIVETO MAGGIORE

Leaving the Via Cassia in Buonconvento (see 2nd tour), we turn left and, on a cart-road of 9 km., we reach **Monteoliveto Maggiore**. The origins of this famous Abbey date back to 1313, when Bernardo dei Tolomei (his given name was Giovanni), who had brought honour to the Sienese University as a lecturer of Law, retired to the lonely «desert of Accona» with two young Sienese noblemen, Ambrogio Piccolomini and Patrizio Patrizi, as a penance. Very soon however, when word of their exemplary solitary life spread, more persons joined them so that in 1319 a new Congregation was established, based on the Benedictine Rule and devoted to S. Maria di Monte Oliveto. Bernardo ended his life in a coherent way, dying from the plague in 1348, together with 80 of his brothers, in Siena, where he had come to assist those already struck by the epidemic. His Congregation, however, continued to develop even after his death and its monasteries had reached the number of 83 by the 18th century, when the suppressions began, which were to decree their abrogation from 1771 to 1870. The buildings of the Chapter House became State property and were declared of high historical and artistic value: in 1876, however, a small Olivetan community was started again in Settignano and, after World War I, monks returned to Monteoliveto as Guests and Custodians of the Archicenoby, now counting 24 monasteries. According to the tradition of the Benedictine Order, the Olivetan Congregation was also a fervent artistic and cultural centre: Olivetan art reached its highest

development in the 15th and 16th cent., while many monks became established in science, literature and music over the two following centuries. Tolomei was beatified in 1644 and the Olivetan St. Francesca Romana (1384-1440) was canonized in 1604.

The imposing abbatial group of buildings, made of fired bricks, rises in the middle of a wide and thick wood of cypress and spruce trees, planted by monks on an area which was once a barren and desolate land, among erosion furrows and steep ravines where the first hermits probably dug their ascetic abodes. We enter the group of buildings through a big vault beside a massive, large tower

framing. Those by Sodoma, painted shortly after the cycle of Camprena (see 2nd tour), mark the painter's splendid development which brought to his maturity in the field of frescoes. In them he developed the fresh and detailed northern naturalism of the late 15th cent., in which his education was deeply rooted, into emerging forms and into a unity and an extent of spaces which are typical of the 16th century, interpreting it at the same time through a fascinating richness and liveliness of narration themes, where characters are depicted by means of a penetrating realistic and psychological insight. Particularly significant are the solemn architectural sceneries, the pleasant landscapes shading off into light-blue far distances in which a personal interpretation of Perugino's sense of space is given, and the imaginative «grotesques» elements dividing the stories. On pilasters looking onto the square are figures of *Hermits* by Mariano di Matteo from Rome, who, in 1474 began the decoration of the cloister; some of those figures were covered by monochrome paintings by Solimena and other 18th-cent. painters. At the end of the cloister is an arch with a nearby scene of *St. Benedict handing over the Rule to the Olivetan* and, on the piers, a *Cross-bearing Christ* and a *Christ by the column* by Sodoma. We enter a room called «De Profundis» since it was used as a tomb for monks, with walls frescoed with scenes of *Hermit fathers of the desert* made of green earth, dated 1440 and partly attrib. to Giovanni di Paolo. Then there is a graceful *Virgin with Child* of marble, dated 1490 and attrib. to brother Giovanni da Verona although showing a marked influence of Antonio Rossellino.
Now we enter the church, completely

restored, to which a deep polygonal apse and a dome with elegant and sober Baroque forms were added from 1772 to 1778 by architect Giov. Antonio Antinori from Camerino. On the nave's ceiling is a fresco representing the *Vision of Blessed Bernardo* by Ermengildo Costantini from Rome (1785) and, over the high altar, a *Virgin's Nativity*, a signed replica by the Veronese Jacopo Ligozzi (1598) who later moved to Florence. At the transept ends are two big canvases representing the *Clothing of the Order's founders* and the *Consecration of the Abbey* by the Sienese Francesco Vanni. The chapel which was added to the right transept wing contains a wooden *Crucifix* which, according to tradition, spoke to Blessed Bernardo. The most important work of art in the whole church, however, is the *wooden choir*, carved and inlaid by the Olivetan brother Giovanni da Verona: with its 48 backs, bearing views of towns, landscapes, church instruments and objects (18 of them from 1503-05 and 30 from 1511-16), it is one of the greatest masterpieces in Renaissance marquetry work. The reading-desk in the middle is by brother Raffaele da Brescia (1520) and the stained-glass windows are by Lino Dinetto (ca. 1699). Back at the cloister, we enter, through the south wing, into the «middle cloister», from which, climbing a stair-case with, on its first landing, a *Crowning of the Virgin* frescoed by Sodoma, we go up to the Library before which is a vestibule with encaustic works by brother Antonio Müller from Danzig (1631) and a sumptuous *candelabrum* engraved by brother Giovanni da Verona (1502). The library is a large hall with three aisles attrib. to brother Giovanni da Verona similar to the one of S. Marco made by Michelozzo in Florence

and in its middle are glass-cases containing precious miniated codices of the 15th cent. coming from the convent of Montemorcino near Perugia. At the end of the hall is the pharmacy, richly furnished with 15th-cent. ceramic pots bearing the Olivetan emblem (three hills with two olive branches). In other rooms of the monastery are frescoes and panel paintings among which a *Madonna* after which a follower of Duccio, the «Maestro di Monteoliveto» was named.

PIENZA

From here, which rises on a high hill overlooking the wide Val d'Orcia. The town is called after the great pope and humanist Pius II (Enea Silvio Piccolomini) who turned the district of Corsignano, where he was born on 18 October 1405, into a small town which ranks today among the best preserved townplanning examples of the Renaissance, rich in admirable buildings and works of art. After his election as a Pope (19.8.1458), Pius II commissioned the renewal of Pienza to Bernardo Rossellino, a Florentine architect who built the Cathedral and Piccolomini Palace, and forced his dignitaries and several private citizens to build their own residences. Meanwhile, 12 houses were being built under the direction of Pietro Paolo del Porrina. Works were started in 1459 and interrupted on the Pope's death (14.8.1464) when Pienza, declared town by a bull of 13 August 1462, had already reached its unmistakable look. The town, surrounded by the medieval walls of old Corsignano, which were reinforced in the 15th cent., is centred around Piazza Pio II onto which the its main buildings look with an admirable harmony of proportions. Two sides of the rectangular-shaped square are diverging, thereby creating two light corridors between which the façade of the CATHEDRAL OF S.M. ASSUNTA stand out beautifully, made of travertine and arranged on two orders, the upper of which shows powerful blind arches inspired by L.B. Alberti's style. The church, crowned by a tympanum having in its middle the pontifical emblem of Pius II, was built from 1459 to 1462 by Rossellino but the ground at the back of the building began to sink a few decades after it was completed, so that complicated foundation works had to be carried out over consecutive periods. The interior, with a nave

Monteoliveto Maggiore: 1. The Big Cloister. Pienza: 2. The Cathedral's apse and belltower; 3. 5. The Cathedral: a remarkable «Assumption of the Virgin and four Saints», masterpiece by Vecchietta.

octagonal bell tower of travertine: the church has crypt which contains a baptismal font planned by Rossellino.

On the right of the square is the grandiose PICCOLOMINI PALACEby Rossellino, inspired by Palazzo Rucellai made by Alberti in Florence, with a beautiful courtyard through which we enter a wonderful hanging garden: this stretches from the front of the palace, with three orders of loggias, to the edge of a hill facing the wonderful landscape of the Val d'Orcia up to the Mount Amiata.

Inside the palace (now property of the Società di Esecutori di Pie Disposizioni di Siena) are a large armoury, the bedroom of Pius II with a bed of the late 16th cent., several rooms with old furnishings and paintings and, on the ground floor, a Library with incunabula, bulls

and two aisles and vaults of the same height, reminding of the «Hallenkirchen» Pius II had admired during his journeys to Germany, is flooded by the light pouring in through the big apsidal windows: light is in fact the main expressive element in the church and it takes on the value of symbol and reality of divine light as theorized by philosophers and theologians. The originality of tetrastyle pilasters should particularly be noted, supporting double pulvins which resemble those in the prolongation of the Sienese Duomo: an admirable solution is also that of the terminal part of the church, with a polygonal plan, where two chapels, in sunburst arrangement, flank the choir and create a continuity with the two ones at the ends of the slightly protruding transept. The panel paintings, all carried out from 1461 to 1464, are characterized by a common devotional and iconographical concept and were painted by the best Sienese painters of those days. On the right, *Virgin with Child and 4 Saints* by Giovanni di Paolo, *Virgin with Child and 4 Saints* by Matteo di Giovanni and, left, an admirable *Assumption of the Virgin and 4 Saints*, masterpiece of Vecchietta, *Virgin with Child and 4 Saints* by Sano di Pietro and again *Virgin with Child and 4 Saints* by Matteo di Giovanni. In the chapel to the right of the choir is a marble altar attrib. to Rossellino: it contains the Head of St. Andrea Apostle inside a beautiful *Reliquiary-bust* of gilded silver commissioned in 1463 by Pius II to the pontifical goldsmith Simone di Giovanni Ghini from Florence, formerly in the Vatican and donated in 1964 to the Cathedral of Pienza by Paul VI to replace an old reliquiary given back to the church of Patrasso. The choir has two orders of seats in Gothic style and is dated 1462. On the left side of the Cathedral is a beautiful

issued by Pius II, rare works of art and a collection of medals. On the square, beside the palace, is a typical WELL planned by Rossellino. In front of the Cathedral are the travertine TOWN HALL, whose façade has a wide portico and four two-light mullioned windows, flanked by a tower of bricks, and AMMANNATI PALACE, commissioned by Card. Giacomo Ammannati, with Guelph windows and raised to the left in the shape of a large tower. On the left side of the piazza are the EPISCOPAL PALACE, originally a Gothic structure transformed by Card. Rodrigo Borgia (later Pope Alexander VI), and the HOUSE OF CANONS, also of the 15th century, the seat of *Museum of the Cathedral*.

The avenue ends at the 14th-century PORTA AL PRATO and, beyond Piazza Pio II, it continues with, at its right, the small PALACE OF CARD. ATREBATENSE and the small PALACE OF CARD. GONZAGA both of the 15th cent., until it reaches PORTA AL CIGLIO in the old town wall. About one km. beyond the gate is the PARISH OF CORSIGNANO, devoted to the SS. Vito and Modesto, a Romanesque building (11th-12th cent.) with a sculptured portal flanked by a peculiarly squat, cylindrical bell tower partly occupying the church interior: on the right is another portal having unrefined Romanesque figures on the architrave. In the church, with a nave and two aisles divided by large pilasters, is a rough font were Pius II and probably Pius III were baptized.

About 7 km. away from Pienza is the Olivetan MONASTERY OF S. ANNA IN CAMPRENA, founded in 1324 by Blessed Bernardo Tolomei, in the refectory of which is the first cycle of frescoes by Sodoma painted in 1503-4 and representing the *Miracle of the loaves*, *St. Benedict in his pontifical authority blessing the Oli-*

vetan Constitutions, a *Mourning over dead Jesus* and *St. Anne, the Virgin and Child blessing two Olivetan monks*. On the wall in front of the windows is a beautiful grotesque frieze with busts of Saints inside medallions and 5 monochrome *Stories of St. Anne*.

MONTEPULCIANO

We leave Pienza, on a road winding among beautiful landscapes, and, after 13 km., we reach **Montepulciano**, at about 600 mt. above sea level, in a wonderful position overlooking the low Val d'Orcia and the Trasimeno lake. The centre, of Etruscan origin (legends report Porsenna as its founder), was fiercely disputed first between Arezzo and Siena, and later between Siena and Florence. It reached its days of splendour when the Medici were readmitted into Florence, and this is why many of its numerous palaces are often true examples of the elegant and austere style of the early 16th-century in Florence. The great poet and humanist Angiolo Ambrosini, called, after his native place, «Poliziano», was born here in 1454.

At the foot of the hill on which the town rises, a short tree-lined avenue to the left leads to the TEMPLE OF S. BIAGIO, one of the most grandiose works of architecture of the whole Renaissance, planned by Antonio da Sangallo the Older, who worked at it from 1519 to 1526. Its plan, with the form of a Greek cross, with dome, apse and two square bell towers on the sides of the façade (one of which is unfinished) develops the Classical ideas conceived by Bramante for St. Peter's and, through the power of structures and the cohesion of wall masses,

adds to the plasticism of structural volumes. The interior is as beautiful as the outside, and perhaps still more imposing, since the walls as a whole form a sort of huge base for the magnificent rhythm of arches which is stressed by large lacunar bands admirably enhancing the dynamism of the building. In front of the church, on the lonely grass lawn surrounding it, is the House of Canons, with a portico and a loggia, built in 1595 after a plan by Sangallo himself, also the author of the puteal on the other side. On a tree-lined avenue about 2 km-long we go up to the town entering through PORTA AL PRATO, a gate opened in the walls of the powerful fortress built for Cosimo I de' Medici by Antonio da Sangallo the Younger: on the opposite square is the *Church of S. Agnese* of the 14th cent., rebuilt in the 17th cent., devoted to the Dominican St. Agnese Segni of Montepulciano (died 1317). Its modern façade has a 14th-century portal and inside the church are two frescoes of the 13th cent., a *Martyrdom of St. Biagio* by Giovanni da S. Giovanni (1619) and a *Nativity of Mary* by Francesco Vanni. Past Porta al Prato, Via Roma leads to a small square where a column supporting a Florentine lion stands: to the left, on the adjacent Piazza Savonarola, is the small, elegantly Baroque church of ST. BERNARDO, which has an oval plan by P. Andrea Pozzo. From Via Roma, which runs through the town for its whole length, we admire an imposing series of 16th-century palaces, the most important of which are: on the right AVIGNONESI PALACE, with façade of travertine, in front of which is TARUGI PALACE, on three storeys, both attrib. to Vignola; further on, to the right, BUCELLI PALACE whose base is dotted with funeral urns and Etruscan and Latin inscriptions. Past the palace is the CHURCH OF S. AGOSTINO, with a beautiful façade by Michelozzo, still late Gothic in the lower part and with Renaissance style in the upper one: in the portal lunette is a terracotta group by the same author. In the interior, reduced and modified during the 18th cent., a *St. Nicola of Tolentino* (formerly in St. Bernardino), a panel painting by Giovanni di Paolo, *Crucifix betw. the Virgin and Magdalene* attrib. to Lorenzo di Credi, *Resurrection of Lazarus* by Alessandro Allori, *Virgin of the Belt* by Barocci and, over the high altar, a beautiful wooden *Crucifix* sculptured by Antonio da Sangallo the Older. In front of the church is the *Clock tow-*

Pienza: 1. Town Hall. Montepulciano: 2. Town Hall; 3. The Cathedral; 4. High Altar: Triptych of the Assumption, by Taddeo di Bartolo.

er with a popular Punchinello striking the hours; then we reach the *Market Loggias* attrib. to Ippolito Scalza: here the road takes on the name of Via Cavour onto which looks, to the left, the unfinished CERVINI PALACE with its two protruding lateral wings in daring arrangement, which Antonio da Sangallo the Older planned for Pope Marcellus II of the Cervini family. Further ahead, on the same side, is GRUGNI PALACE with a beautiful ashlar portal attrib. to Vignola, followed, after Palace of the Seminary, by the CHURCH OF GESU', with an elegant, circular-shaped interior after a plan by P.Andrea Pozzo, finished in 1733 with statues of stucco attrib. to Bartolomeo Mazzuoli. The road, continuing with the names of Via Garibaldi and Via Poliziano - the house of the poet standing on its left - ends with the 14th-century CHURCH OF S. MARIA DEI SERVI in whose very elegant Baroque interior, restored by Andrea Pozzo, a *Virgin with Child* by Ugolino di Nerio is preserved. From there, on the road which runs round the FORTEZZA MEDICEA, a fortress rebuilt in false Gothic style, and on the Via Firenzuola (we see on the left the house where Card. Roberto Bellarmino was born in 1532), we reach the main square, the highest point of the town where the Cathedral, the Town Hall and other beautiful palaces stand. The Cathedral was built between 1592 and 1630 after a plan by Ippolito Scalza and its rough façade is flanked by an unfinished bell tower of the 15th century. The interior, in the shape of a Latin cross, with a nave and two aisles, is wide and bright and its structures have very noble outlines. To the left of the entrance is the lying statue of *Bartolomeo Aragazzi* formerly belonging to a magnificent mausoleum which Michelozzo Michelozzi sculptured between 1427 and 1436 for the secretary of Martin V: the famous monument, one of the masterpieces of 15th-century sculpture, was dismembered during the 17th cent., and its most important pieces are displayed inside the Cathedral: two beautiful reliefs of the front walled up by the first two pilasters, two grandiose statues of *Faith* and *Science* on both sides of the high altar and *St. Bartholomew* at the beginning of the transept left wing. Over the high altar is an imposing triptych (the biggest work of the whole Sienese painting school) with *Assumption* by Taddeo di Bartolo (1401) and, by the two pilasters in the middle of the cross-vault are two delicate wooden statues of *Annunciating angel* and *Annunciated Virgin* attrib. to Francesco di Valdambrino. In the first chapel to the left, used as baptistery, are a beautiful *altarpiece* of glazed terra-cotta by the

3

4

school of Andrea della Robbia and a *baptismal font* by Giovanni d'Agostino (ca.1340). The TOWN HALL, of the 2nd half of the 14th cent., has a façade planned by Michelozzo (1424) characterized by a high tower in the middle with double embattlement: its small courtyard with different orders of loggias is of the 14th century. On the opposite side of the square is CONTUCCI PALACE (formerly *Del Monte*) begun in 1519 by Antonio da Sangallo the Older and finished in the 18th cent.: on the left is TARUGI PALACE (formerly *Nobili*), the most beautiful in town, probably planned by Vignola, with loggia and arcade. Not far from here is the WELL OF GRIFFINS AND LIONS of 1520; on one corner of the square is the PALACE OF THE CAPITANO DEL POPOLO, whose ogival side looks onto Via Ricci. Here, on the left, are RICCI PALACE, attrib. to Peruzzi, and, to the right, NERI ORSELLI PALACE, the seat of the CIVIC MUSEUM. Through a vestibule with small genre paintings of different periods, we enter a little hall with two *altar frontals*, a *lunette* and a *Baptist* by Andrea della Robbia, then a hall with paintings of different periods and schools, even foreign ones, partly coming from a collection of the Crociani canons, some of which are attrib. to Bronzino, Manetti, Spagnoletto, Spadarino, Giusto Sustermans, etc.. On the upper floor, in a single hall, are: a *St. Francis* by Margarito d'Arezzo, a *Virgin betw. two Angels* by the school of Duccio, a *Crucifixion* by Luca di Tommè, a radiant *Crowning of the Virgin* by Jacopo di Mino del Pellicciaio, an *Adoration of the Child* by Girolamo di Benvenuto, a *Magdalene* by Cigoli and other remarkable paintings, while a glass case contains a collection of miniated choir-books of Byzantine school from the 15th century. Via Ricci ends at one side of the 13th-century CHURCH OF S. FRANCESCO still preserving on the outside the remains of a pulpit from which St. Bernardino preached: in the restored interior, inside a chapel to the left, is a false polyptych fresco of 14th-cent. Sienese school. On the left of the church a beautiful view of the surrounding countryside is offered, with the underlying church of S. Biagio. Going down Via Mazzini we reach the graceful CHURCH OF S. LUCIA with a Baroque façade by Flaminio del Turco (in the interior, *Virgin with Child* by Signorelli) and, on Via Saffi, we return to the Market Loggias.

CHIANCIANO

Down to the crossroads of S. Biagio we turn left and, after ca. 8 km., we reach **Chianciano**. On the left rises

1

Chianciano vecchio, of Etruscan origin, partly surrounded by medieval walls. We enter the town through PORTA RIVELLINI and, on the left, we see the small CHURCH OF MISERICORDIA (in the interior, *sinopite* attrib. to Signorelli); going along the main road we reach MANENTI CASTLE and the CLOCK TOWER, both medieval and restored; further ahead, on Via Solferino, we come to a small square on which the 13th-cent. PALACE OF THE PODESTÀ and the *Arcipretura* look, the latter containing a small MUSEUM OF SACRED ART. It contains a *Painted cross* by a follower of Duccio («Maestro di S. Polo in Rosso»), a *polyptych* after which the «Maestro di Chianciano» is named, the unrefined follower of Duccio, a stained-glass window with *St. John the Baptist* of 15th-cent. Florentine school, a wooden *Madonna* by an artist close to Arnolfo di Cambio, a *Virgin with Child* attrib. to Lorenzo di Niccolò di Martino (early 15th cent.), vestments, choir-books, small urns and Etruscan fragments. Not far from here is the COLLEGIATE CHURCH OF S. GIOVANNI BATTISTA of the 13th cent., with original portal and an interior restructured in Neoclassical style in 1809: in it are a *Nativity Scene* by Rustichino (17th cent.) and a wooden *Crucifix* of the 14th century. Starting from the Collegiate, and going down Via della Croce, we reach the *Porta del Sole* beyond which is the beautiful CHURCH OF MADONNA DELLA ROSA, «the humble sister of S. Biagio in Montepulciano», in the shape of a Greek cross, built in 1585 after an unfinished plan by Baldassarre Lanci from Urbino.

About 3 km. away from old Chianciano rises **CHIANCIANO TERME**, one of the most important and frequented spas in Italy, a modern-looking resort made mainly of hotels and boarding-houses. The hot spring waters of Chianciano, which have been well-known since ancient times (a stone inscription of the 17th cent. even counts them «inter celebres delicias» of Etruscan Porsenna), when they were called «Balnea Clusina» and remembered by Horace, and which were also popular throughout the Middle Ages, still prove to be an effective treatment against all hepatobiliary and metabolism disorders, as well as against cardiovascular and urinary tract diseases.

CHIUSI

Through Viale Baccelli we take the road to **Chiusi**, about 13 km. away from Chianciano Terme, a very old town which was once one of the most powerful of the twelve Etruscan «lucumonie»: its original name was *Chamars*, later Latinized into *Clusium*.

Chiusi was remembered by Virgil in his Aeneid as one of the Etruscan towns which helped Aeneas against Turnus, king of the Latins, and its history reports important events after Rome's foundation, when «lucumon» Porsenna, taking the opportunity to reinstate back to power the dethroned Tarquinius the Proud, besieged Rome and most probably even conquered it (520 B.C.). Later, however, when his son Arunte, sent by him to conquer the Roman town of Aricia, was defeated and killed, Porsenna found it profitable to be reconciled with Rome and to return to Chiusi where he died after years of enlightened government. In 391 B.C. Chiusi was invaded and destroyed by the Senones Gauls, led by Brennus, and in 296 it entered the Roman alliance, even if old traditions and the Etruscan language were preserved there until very late. In 82 B.C. Sulla set up a colony in Chiusi; Christianity must have spread there quite early, as is proved by two Christian catacombs and by its becoming an episcopal seat in the 4th century. After being occupied by the Goths it was conquered by the Langobards in the late 6th cent. who established there a dukedom which was abolished in 776. Later on, Chiusi was governed by a series of Gastaldi, replaced, in the late 9th cent., by Counts, whose powers extended on a wide area over the surrounding territory. Towards the 11th cent., however, malaria caused its decline, also described by Dante

Chianciano: 1. Renaissance Fountain; in the background Clock Tower. Chiusi: 2. Porta Lavinia; 3. Frescoes of the Estruscan tomb called Tomba del Colle; 4. Frescoes of the Etruscan Monkey Tomb.

(Paradise, XVI, 75). During the 12th cent. it was ruled by Orvieto and passed under the jurisdiction of Siena in 1231. After the occupation of the Ghibelline troops of Lapo Farinata degli Uberti in 1283 and of Napoleone Orsini, the Pope's legate, in 1307, Chiusi was disputed between Perugia and Orvieto and had a self-government as a City-State until 1355, when Charles IV appointed there one of his officers. Again under the Sienese domination in 1380, the town was occupied in 1414 by Attendolo Sforza who sold it back to Siena two years later for 18,000 golden florins. From then on the history of Chiusi was always linked to Siena. After coming under the rule of Florence in 1556, the town began to flourish again thanks to massive reclamation activities in the Val di Chiana, fostered by Cosimo I de' Medici and continued by his successors. The famous monk Graziano, founder of Canon Law and author of the well-known collection of laws called «*Decretum Gratiani*» was born in Chiusi.

We enter the town through Porta Cavallotti, a gate leading into Via Porsenna. Past the small Piazza Graziano, on which a column supporting an emblem of the Medici family stands (1581), on the left is BONCI-CASUCCINI PALACE with a 15th-century façade and, further ahead, on the right, DELLA CIAIA PALACE with an adjoining small palace of the 14th cent.; then we reach Piazza del Duomo with a massive defence tower of the 12th cent. in its middle, turned into a bell tower in 1595 (under the tower is a big bathing pool of the 1st cent. B.C., with two naves of tufa and covered by two pointed domes). The CATHEDRAL (S. Secondiano) was built in the 2nd half of the 5th cent. on the model of early Christian basilicas and was partly rebuilt during the 12th cent., when its aisles were raised, and again in 1887-94 by architect Giuseppe Partini, the author of the arcade which runs by the façade.

Adjoining the cathedral is a small *Museum* which contains a precious collection of 22 choir-books coming from the Abbey of Monte Oliveto Maggiore and donated to the Chapter in 1810.

Roman inscriptions connects the Cathedral to the EPISCOPAL PALACE, enlarged in the 19th cent. and, in front of its left side, is the ETRUSCAN NATIONAL MUSEUM, established in 1870 and later extended and enriched.

Of minor importance are other town churches, among which is the Romanesque one of S. FRANCESCO and that of S. MARIA DELLA MORTE, both of the 13th cent. although with restored interiors. Our visit, however, continues in

Piazza Vittorio Veneto, once a foot-ball field, now rearranged as a public garden with archaeological remains among flower-beds: on one side of it are walls and a large tower of a 12th-cent. FORTRESS. To complete the visit to the museum we have to take a walk into the nearby streets where a number of **Etruscan tombs** can be seen. Differently from other Etruscan towns, Chiusi does not have a real necropolis, whereas tombs, discovered in various periods, are scattered on the surrounding countryside, so that a visit to them will take some time. A usually recommended tour is that to the tombs of Grand Duke, Monkey and Pellegrina, all of them lying beyond the railway.

INDEX

SIENA

Legend:

1. Piazza del Campo (Square of the Field)
2. National Picture Gallery - *Via S. Pietro 29*
3. Church of S. Pietro alle Scale - *Via S. Pietro*
4. Prato S. Agostino - *corner Via S. Agata - Via A. Mattioli*
5. Cathedral - Museum of the Metropolitan Institution - crypt - Baptistery - *Piazza Duomo*
6. Piazza del Mercato (Market square)
7. Church of Santa Maria dei Servi - *Piazza A. Manzoni*
8. Church of S. Spirito - *Piazza S. Santo Spirito*
9. Church of S. Giorgio - *Via Banchi di Sotto*
10. Church of S. Martino - *Via Banchi di Sotto*
11. Logge del Papa - *Via Banchi di Sotto*
12. Piccolomini Palace - *Via Banchi di Sotto*
13. Church of S. Maria di Provenzano - *Piazza Provenzano*
14. Basilica of S. Francesco - *Piazza S. Francesco*
15. Ex-convent of S. Francesco - *Piazza S. Francesco*
16. Church of S. Donato - *Piazza Abbadia*
17. Salimbeni Palace - *Piazza Salimbeni*
18. Tolomei Palace - *Via Banchi di Sopra*
19. Church of S. Cristoforo - *Piazza Tolomei*
20. Branda Fountain - *Via Fonte Branda*
21. Sanctuary of S. Caterina - *Via del Tiratoio 15*
22. Church of S. Giuseppe - *Via S. Agata*
23. Basilica of S. Domenico - *Piazza S. Domenico*
24. Church of S. Niccolò al Carmine - *Piano dei Mantellini*
25. Hospital of S. Maria della Scala and the National Archeological Museum (being transferred) - *Piazza Duomo*

Printed in April 1989 by
LA FOTOMETALGRAFICA EMILIANA SPA
San Lazzaro di Savena - Bologna